WINNING CUSTODY

DEEDRA B. HUNTER, M.S., L.M.H.C.

WITH TOM MONTE

 ST. MARTIN'S GRIFFIN ❦ NEW YORK

WINNING CUSTODY

A WOMAN'S GUIDE TO RETAINING

CUSTODY OF HER CHILDREN

www.stmartins.com

Book design by Victoria Kuskowski

ISBN 0-312-25265-X

First Edition: January 2001

10 9 8 7 6 5 4 3 2 1

To my three wonderful and courageous children,

Rob, Brandon, and Kristina.

Thank you for being born. I love you.

CONTENTS

ACKNOWLEDGMENTS

I cannot present this book without first acknowledging my immense gratitude to those who were instrumental in helping me retain custody of my children and then assisting me in the creation of this book. No one makes it through the ordeal of a custody suit and then successfully writes about it without a great deal of help. The people listed here gave me that help in abundance.

Let me begin by thanking attorney Frank Abrams, who helped me both with my custody suit as well as with the writing of this book. Frank Abrams is not only a man of tremendous knowledge and wisdom, but also one of extremely high ethics, tremendous sensitivity, and kindness. Not only do you know the letter of the law, Frank, but also its spirit. Thank you for all that you have done for me.

Thank you, Dr. Michael Lerner, for your support, intelligence, and wisdom. Thanks, especially, for being at my side when the chips were down on that long Sunday in front of the judge.

Thank you, Dr. Linda Keller, for the loving care you gave my children during an extremely difficult period in their lives.

Three special women deserve my heartfelt gratitude for the care and kindness they gave my children: Terry Dominquez, Glenna Payne Jones, and Carol Haverfield Mann. Without you, life would have been utter chaos.

Many teachers and staff at the David Fairchild Elementary School in South Miami, Florida, gave their support, care, and kindness to my children when they needed it most. Thank you all.

Thank you, Sophie, for helping organize my family diary and for giving so freely of your superb legal and secretarial skills.

Thank you, Robbie Burns, for being my friend, coach, and

inspiration. You are the "can do" voice that I still hear singing in my ears.

Thank you, Jennifer Nichols Kennedy, for traveling to Miami from Orlando on so many occasions to testify on my behalf. Your support and generosity went way beyond the call.

Janise O'Hara walked the last mile with me when I was most exhausted. Thank you for your humor, care, and perspective. You were a constant reminder that sanity would eventually prevail.

Thank you, Carol Gallelli. Your support, business acumen, and counseling skills have made you the perfect Custody Coach partner. Thank you, as well, for your patience and all your assistance in helping me rejoin the world and trust again.

Thank you, Diana Kwatra, M.H.A., M.S., A.R.N.P., and Barbara Tashkin, for your love and understanding.

To the staff at the Winter Park YMCA, thank you for creating a warm and friendly place where the only discomforts were those encountered on your wonderful exercise equipment.

A very special thanks to Tom Monte for helping me tell my story. I will forever be grateful.

Finally, to my editor at St. Martin's Press, Heather Jackson, and her assistant, Ellen Smith, thank you for your faith in this book and for allowing me to help women who face custody suits, a time when every ounce of support really counts.

FOREWORD

When Deedra Hunter first came to my office in late 1995, little did I know that her experiences would later take the form of a book. It's a book for which I'm proud to say a few words.

As an attorney for many years, practicing primarily in the field of family law, I have had mothers and fathers coming to me with burdens that seem insurmountable. They are in anguish over the power of judges to decide the issue of custody for their sons and daughters. And they are distraught by a system of representation where lawyers many times do not have their clients' best interests at heart.

This book ought to be a national bestseller, and it should be on the shelf of every parent. Friends should buy this book for anyone they know who is going through a custody-related court matter.

Over the years, I have been witness to some of the most heart-wrenching cases you can imagine. It is no secret that around the country family and custody issues are flooding the courts. Many judges do not have the time or the will to familiarize themselves with any one specific case. Further, serious additional problems are raised through the system of legal representation. Lawyers are paid by the hour, and, as you can guess, there can be a strong incentive on the part of some (not all) lawyers to complicate, purposefully or negligently, what otherwise might be a simple case matter. All the while, the fear, anxiety, and heartache on the part of the parents and, more important, on the part of the children continues.

This book addresses issues that you will not learn anywhere else, issues such as how to prepare yourself from the onset for that dreaded thing known as a "custody battle." This includes such important subjects as how to get ready for court, how to present yourself, even how to pick a lawyer.

Deedra Hunter has used her own personal experience, as well as her professional background as a family counselor, to create a book like no other. She tells you how to take control and avoid being a victim of the legal system.

Winning Custody fills a void. It explains things few lawyers will tell you, some of which could be too difficult and painful to learn directly for yourself. It may sound odd, given the subject, to say I hope you enjoy reading this book. By that I mean, and this is most important, that I hope it leads to the peace, tranquillity, and level state of mind lacking so often in individuals involved in custody disputes.

—Frank A. Abrams, Esq.

WINNING CUSTODY

INTRODUCTION

With the exception of the death of her children or the potential loss of her own life, a mother finds nothing more terrifying than the thought of losing her children. Yet women embroiled in child custody suits face that threat every day in American courts. Approximately 1.2 million divorces take place in the United States each year, which, in addition to dividing adults, also separate more than 1 million children from one of their parents. About 150,000 divorcing couples cannot arrive at an amicable arrangement and are forced to ask a court to determine which parent is more qualified to raise their children. A custody case can take two to three years to settle, which means that during any one year, a lot more than 150,000 couples are embroiled in such a suit.

This book is a guide to women who face the terrible trials of a child custody suit. The purpose of this book essentially is fourfold. First and most important, I want to help you win your suit and retain custodial care of your children. Second, I will help you maintain your sanity as you navigate your way through the minefield of trouble you now face, or are about to face. Third, I will support you as you try to be as good a mother as you can be during this extremely difficult time in your life. Fourth, I will help you find the light of peace and forgiveness at the other end of this dark process.

Child custody suits can occur at the time of a divorce, or several years after two people have gone their separate ways. In my own case, I had been divorced for more than two years when my ex-husband decided to sue for custody of our children. The primary difference between these two types of cases—that is, whether the custody suit occurs as part of the divorce or well after the divorce has occurred—is whether there are property issues to be settled as well. It's also true that even when a custody suit takes place well after a divorce has occurred, property disputes may arise and become part of the custody case. No matter what other issues may be involved, you and your former husband must do all you can to separate the child custody issues from any property disputes you may have. Your children must not become objects to be negotiated against property demands. I address those issues in greater depth in Chapter 1.

Much of the trouble you face now flows from feelings and issues left unresolved at the time of your divorce. It's worth considering those issues again *before* you go to court—for the simple reason that they may help the two of you achieve a mutually acceptable agreement before you both inflict tremendous pain on each other and, more important, on your children.

As anyone who has ever separated from a spouse knows, divorce brings with it an avalanche of painful feelings. Whatever was holding your marriage together—memories of love, your willingness to sacrifice yourself for your children, your stubborn attachment to old dreams, simple inertia—eventually gives way. With separation and divorce, you finally accept the terrible reality that all of those unresolved conflicts, unmet needs, and lingering resentments are not going to be resolved. You realize yet again, for the umpteenth time, that there isn't going to be a happy ending to the union you and your husband formed however many years ago. Only this time, the realization is final. Somehow that makes it hurt even more. Your sense of failure may be so great that it forces you to turn inward, isolating you and making you numb to the possibility that a better life awaits you. You are hurt, angry, sad, bitter, and more than a little afraid about what the future may hold. But even worse, you feel wounded and betrayed, not just by your spouse, but by the mistakes you may have made along the way. Your sense of personal failure may be acute. How did I go so wrong? you may be asking yourself. How did I allow things to go so far? Why didn't I leave sooner? Whatever your husband may be saying, you can be sure that he is coping with his own version of this same nightmare.

When people have been defeated and flattened by life, they often do two things. First, it's very common to blame others for our own mistakes. In the case of divorce, this can lead both parties to demonize each other, each seeing the other as the cause of all his or her pain, sadness, and anger. Once you allow yourself to see the other as evil, all kinds of behaviors suddenly become permissible. Unfortunately, these behaviors solve nothing and usually lead to even bigger problems. Second, people commonly grab for anything of value that may still be left on the battlefield. In the aftermath of divorce, the most precious items that still remain are the children.

It is these very conditions that help precipitate a child custody suit.

Custody cases, as I will make clear throughout this book, are complex forms of family mutilation. Whatever volume of pain, torment, and sheer ugliness that you and your former spouse may have inflicted on each other during your marriage and divorce will be multiplied many times over by a custody battle. If you think you know how low your former husband will go—indeed, if you think you know how low you are willing to go—think again. If you enter a custody suit, things will get far worse for both of you.

The trouble is, you and your former husband are not the ones injured most. The biggest victims in all custody battles are the children. As you and your former husband start attacking each other and then escalate hostilities in order to win the battle, your children get caught in the cross fire. Emotionally, they can be torn apart.

Now I know what you're thinking: that you know this already and you're wondering how it can be avoided. Allow me to deal with each of these two points separately.

Even though you may be aware on some level that your children will be hurt the most in this custody thing, you will stop knowing it the moment you enter the fray. Once the battle is joined, the emotional intensity—especially the fear—is heightened to such a degree that it is difficult, sometimes even impossible, to think clearly or rationally. In the maelstrom that follows, your instincts take over. All you want to do at that point is survive the ordeal and walk away from it with custodial care of your children. You will do just about anything to accomplish these goals. You and your former spouse will very likely attack each other over an endless array of character flaws—some of them intensely personal—as each of you attempts to prove that you are the parent with whom your children should live. During this process, which at times can feel like living in an inferno, the children somehow get transformed into objects to be fought over and won. Ask any divorce lawyer and he or she will tell you dozens of horror stories about parents who became so deeply embroiled in their own battle that they lost all awareness of how much they were hurting their children. But if you had asked any of these couples beforehand who would be hurt the most, all of them would have answered, "The children, of course."

After your custody battle is over, you will realize that during the proceedings, some form of madness took hold of you and your former spouse. As you read this book, you will begin to understand why this occurs. My hope is that you'll be able to avoid the worst of it.

Once they enter the fray, however, most parents stop thinking about the health and well-being of their children. They think only of winning. Very often they tell themselves that they must do all they can to win, that the battle is no holds barred, and that they must fight and survive the process. They'll make it up to their children when this is all over.

There are complex reasons for this bizarre behavior, starting with the terrible emotions, especially guilt and failure, let loose in the aftermath of a divorce. Many a parent regards winning custody of their children as a statement by the court that he or she was not at fault in the marriage. The judge validates a person's lack of fault in the situation, in effect saying, Yes, your spouse really *was* impossible to live with. The judge's verdict may even be interpreted to mean that the court finds one parent so inadequate that it cannot turn the children over to him or her.

Victory not only validates but also serves as sweet revenge. The victor—in fact, there are no real winners in this process— has employed one of society's most powerful institutions, the courts, to implement his or her own will. A certain social stamp of approval extends to the spouse who prevails in court. And finally there is the reward, the thing you have fought so hard to gain. Victory means that one of you gains the most precious thing the two of you ever had. It means that one of you can use the verdict as a source of comfort. And it means that one of you will absorb yet another terrible loss.

Both parties know this, at least instinctively, as they go into the proceedings. Hence both parties realize just how high the stakes really are. This, of course, makes the war between the two even more intense and brutal. Many people will stop at nothing to destroy the reputation of their former spouse in the eyes of the court. Former spouses will use financial pressures, sexual histories, and relationships with friends, parents, and former intimate partners to gain an advantage in court. And a great many use the children as pawns in these battles.

During the custody suit, the emotional condition of your life can turn so bleak that it's as if someone important in your life had died. Actually, it's worse than that. The feeling is more like the anticipation of your own death.

Eventually it ends. The court rules and the mandated living arrangements are established. But in the wake of such a battle, the children and their parents are wounded for life. Even the parent who "wins" custody or custodial care sees his or her relationship with the children altered, usually for the worse.

All of which brings us to the question: How do you avoid such a terrible fate? Only one answer will guarantee escape: If it is at all possible, without compromising your position, attempt to settle your case. According to numerous divorce lawyers whom I have consulted and everything that I have read, people are far more satisfied with the settlements they have created themselves than with those mandated by a court.

I realize that these are difficult words to read, especially if you have already tried again and again to reach a peaceful settlement. Many of you will say, "I've already tried that. I've done all that I can to make peace with him and to work out an arrangement beneficial to our children and each of us." If there is even the slightest opportunity to try again, please do. You must do all you can to arrive at a sane and just settlement for your children's sake and your own. If you are able to abort this process, you stand a better chance of achieving a lasting peace that will benefit you and your children.

By doing all you can to avoid a custody suit and then going one step further, you are more likely to be at peace if you are forced to enter a court battle. You will know in your heart that a court-mandated settlement was unavoidable, but that you did everything in your power to avoid it. Then you can enter this process with a certain clarity and conviction, which makes winning custody more likely.

If your husband will not yield custodial care to you and you know in your heart that your children will be better off living with you, then you must go forward. You have no choice but to fight.

It is my intention to help you deal with all that that fight will bring to your life and to your child or children. I want to help you prepare for many of the problems that will arise before, during, and after you are in court. I also want to provide coping skills to deal with unforeseen problems. The book will help you raise your children while the proceedings are under way. It will help you cope with your former spouse. And, I hope, it will help you achieve a peace with yourself and your children.

The first thing you must understand is that the process will change you. It can destroy you, leaving you so wounded and bitter that you emerge as a smaller, weaker version of yourself, or it can transform you for the better. Believe it or not, this process can make you stronger, healthier, and more whole than you were when you first entered these proceedings. As ugly as this process can get, it can serve to make you love and accept yourself more completely.

It did exactly that for me.

Beginning in 1994, my former husband and I engaged in a protracted and vicious custody suit. I am a therapist with more than twenty years of experience in private practice. I knew in advance the potential my former husband and I had for inflicting terrible pain on each other and on our three children. I tried as best I could to avoid such a battle. My efforts failed and we were forced to go to court. Once in court, the door to our private lives was ripped off its hinges and all our secrets were made public. It was a devastating experience. My former spouse sought to portray me as psychologically unfit to be a mother. While this tactic is commonly used in custody battles, it bore a special fear for me.

During my young adulthood and for many years during my marriage I suffered from bulimia. I was afraid some deeper imbalance fueled my bulimia and found myself attracted to certain types of men, men who were often charming on the surface, but suffered from a deep and barely hidden rage. I had long believed that something inside me, something as yet unidentified, was leading me into destructive behaviors and had in fact led me into a very destructive marriage.

Throughout my life, I have been driven to understand myself on a deeper level. The bulimia intensified my desire to seek answers to my inner conflicts. Another driving force was a powerful inner doubt that I had about myself. I had spent most of my adult life in therapy and my counselors assured me of my stability and inner strength. Yet I didn't really believe them. Surely there was something terribly wrong with me, though I couldn't say what it was. Even after I had recovered fully from my bulimia, I continued to engage in therapy.

Despite such fears, I also had a very high-functioning side that was the master of many parts of my life. I am an excellent and a successful therapist. It is said that wounded healers are the best kind, and certainly I qualify as that. Not only do I have empathy and compassion, but I also possess a gift for understanding human nature. This ability emerged during my childhood, when I learned to survive by seeing deeply into my parents and noting the subtle changes that foreshadowed trouble or short periods of peace. By having insight into them and other adults, I was able to adjust my behavior accordingly and survive the emotional upheavals that constantly erupted in our home.

My mother, Anita Boyer, was a singer; my father, Bobby Dukoff, a saxophonist. Both performed with many of the big bands of the 1940s and '50s, among them Glenn Miller and the orchestras of Tommy and Jimmy Dorsey. They had also cut successful records and were noted, if minor stars. My mother was addicted to alcohol and drugs—mostly phenobarbital, a drug similar to Valium—which split her personality in two. Onstage, she was pretty, effervescent, talented, and loving. At home, she was often depressed and angry. As an only child, I was a target for her rage. Nothing I did could gain my mother's approval; when she was drinking or taking drugs, it was even worse. Sometimes she'd criticize my weight, my looks—anything, just to inflict pain, it seemed. My father was a silent partner in all of this, the passive figure who allowed the abuse and sometimes pacified my mother and affected blindness to all she was doing.

I emerged from my family wounded, confused, and very ashamed. The only thing that interested me was psychology, which I studied in high school, college, and graduate school. I was always a good student who excelled in academics, but I was secretly burdened by a terrible shame. Bulimia was the outward symptom of my shame, but it was the shame that was the real illness.

Shame makes a person hide. There are ways of hiding that allow you to keep your secrets, even as you succeed in your public role. I did that with bulimia. I managed to keep it a secret while counseling others, sometimes even people suffering from eating disorders.

I was ashamed of myself because I suspected that there was a problem deeper than the bulimia that I had not yet uncovered. I feared that the custody suit would somehow violently uncover that underlying disorder and cause me to lose my children, a fate that might destroy me. I was terrified of going to court.

Now, at the age of forty-eight, I was finally forced to confront my worst fears. That confrontation would not take place in the safe confines of a therapist's office but in a court of law. My accuser was my former husband, who knew every little secret that I had long tried to keep hidden. The future of my children and, in a very real sense, my very identity hung in the balance.

My former husband and his attorney; the Miami Human Resource Service agents who would grill me on my past; the therapists who would evaluate my psychological competence; and the judge who would assess me and render a verdict formed the gauntlet I was now forced to run. It was the most terrifying experience of my life. It was also my life's defining moment.

The proceedings were even uglier than I had expected. As it turned out, all my hidden demons emerged, in full public view. I had to fight for my life and the lives of my children. My shame surfaced and had to be dealt with openly and honestly. So did my anger. I experienced the discrimination against women by our courts and, by extension, our society. In the process, I had to find my own intelligence, strength, and honesty and use them to fight for what I believed was right.

And I prevailed. On January 19, 1996, the judge ruled that I would retain residential custodial care of my three children. This was the only victory I sought in court. But to my great surprise, I received something more: I had finally integrated my own strength and power. With it came two other characteristics that I had long denied myself: compassion and love. In the course of fighting my own demons, even more than my former husband, I was forced to confront and accept myself. Somehow, in the course of fighting for a just cause, I was able to feel compassion for myself. I saw how difficult my life's path had been and how many obstacles I had overcome. And despite my shortcomings and the difficulties I faced, I had been a dedicated and loving mother to my children. I had done my best.

In my darkest hour, my children came to me and told me how much they loved me. Even more important, they had realized how much I loved them.

The process you may be facing now is cruel and in many ways unjust. Many of us must enter this process and do all we can to emerge with our children and our self-respect. This is no easy task, especially for the woman. So much of a woman's self-esteem is invested in being a good mother. Yet during a custody suit she must prove her worthiness as a mother. After you have made every effort to prove your worth—a task inherently degrading and unseemly—you must then await the judgment of the court. As I said, it is a cruel process, but one that every woman must understand and be savvy about if she is to prevail.

As difficult as this process is, there is a great opportunity implicit in it. You can emerge stronger and wiser. If you use your wisdom and strength in the right way, you will also gain tremendous self-respect and self-love. You will see yourself and your struggle as heroic. Contrary to all that you might believe right now, this experience can lead you to a better life.

The chapters in this book are arranged according to how the events normally unfold in the custody process. The first chapter is a guide to finding the right lawyer and confronting the legal questions you will face. This is the first task you must perform and one of the most important in the process.

Once you have a lawyer and some of the shock has worn off, you must face the fact that you will be defending your mothering, an endeavor filled with many misunderstandings and guilt. Chapter 2 deconstructs the perfect mother image and helps you honor yourself and the mother you have been.

Chapter 3 shows you how to document your role as mother—an essential task as you try to prove your worthiness as a parent.

Chapter 4 shows you how you can cope with the fear of losing your children and how to get the support you need.

Chapter 5 gives you insights into what your children need and how you can best meet those needs.

Chapter 6 advises you on how to deal with your former husband.

Chapter 7 shows you how to handle the family court service personnel and psychologists.

Chapter 8 advises you on how to present yourself in court.

Chapter 9 gives you guidance on how you can start the healing process and take up the first steps toward forgiveness.

In each of the chapters, I provide some of my own experiences as an example—very often an example of what *not* to do. As I relate these experiences, I am also trying to familiarize you with the situations you are likely to encounter. I hope that by doing this I will better prepare you for what lies ahead.

It is my hope that this book will help guide you to a successful conclusion of your custody suit and to a new and rewarding relationship with your children and a better relationship with yourself.

1 HOW TO FIND THE RIGHT LAWYER

On August 14, 1994, a man from Miami's Dade County Sheriff's Department rang my doorbell and presented me with a set of legal documents that informed me that I was being sued by my former husband for custody of our three children. I had been divorced for more than two and a half years. As part of the divorce settlement, we had agreed that I would have custodial care of our children and that he would have liberal visitation rights, which he exercised without any restrictions by me. I had no forewarning that a suit was in the offing. This turn of events came as a complete shock to me.

As I looked at the pages, an electric fear ran through my body until it rattled all my nerves and blurred my vision. I went into the living room, sat down on my couch, and tried to get a grip on myself. The man from the sheriff's office followed me. "What does this mean?" I asked the process server.

"He's suing you for custody of your children," he said, making no effort to hide the embarrassment and apology in his voice. He looked around the living room and then said awkwardly, "You have a really nice home. I'm sorry to have to deliver this bad news to you."

"Thank you," I said as if to myself. I was still looking at the paperwork, but not seeing the words. There was a long gap in which nothing was said. Finally the man said that I had to sign a page to acknowledge receipt of the documents. "I'm sorry," I said. " I guess I'm in shock." I signed the papers and showed him to the door.

Everything will be all right, I kept telling myself. But inside I knew that a lot of trouble was brewing. I was possessed by fear, too numb even to cry.

Until my doorbell had rung, the day had been utterly normal. I am a psychotherapist with a busy practice. Earlier in the day, I had seen several clients. Normally, I come home in the afternoon to be with my children and make dinner arrangements for everyone. I do not cook. Ever since I was a child, I have had a very conflicted relationship with food, and when I was twenty-four I developed bulimia, which would last for the next sixteen years. Now, at the age of forty-eight, I had been free of the disorder for eight years, but I was still unable to prepare real meals like most mothers. Instead, I kept easy-to-prepare breakfast and luncheon foods in the house and ordered our dinners out. On this August day, my two younger children, Brandon, then twelve, and Kristina, then ten, were outside playing with friends. My oldest son, Rob, then fourteen, was with his father on a camping trip, which somehow made the receipt of these legal documents all the more threatening. I wanted to gather them in my arms and protect us all from the storm on the horizon.

I felt more alone than I had ever been in my life. In the time it took to read a single page, written of course in the most threatening language of all, the lawyer's tongue, I was engulfed by real terror. He's got a lawyer and they're going to take me to court, I said to myself. They're going to do everything they can to take my children away from me. They're going to attack and embellish every flaw in my character, every mistake I have ever made. What am I going to do? What can I do? I've got to get a lawyer. Whom can I call? Where do I find the right one? Can I even afford a lawyer? Can I defend myself against all that he knows?

Similar questions probably popped into your mind on the terrible day when the bad news arrived, or may still be haunting you if you are still at the outset of your custody suit. Whether you realize it or not, this is one of the most dangerous moments in the entire child custody process. What you do after you receive those papers will determine to a great extent the tone, character, and outcome of your custody battle. It will determine how much the suit costs you, and how you and your children are affected by this process. In other words, once you receive the papers, you are vulnerable. Be careful. Don't do anything until you understand all that you are facing and what every step in the process will mean.

The first thing you must do is hire an attorney to represent you. Before you start calling friends, relatives, or the local bar association for referrals, you must understand how much your attorney can influence what you face, for good or ill. In fact, this knowledge should help you determine which lawyer you choose to represent you. In this chapter, I want to tell you what you need to know before you start interviewing lawyers. Right now, you may think that this battle is exclusively between you and your former husband. It's not. The battle is often four-sided. The contestants are you, your former husband, your lawyer, and his lawyer.

In a very real sense, you and your former husband can become pawns of your respective attorneys, who may have their own objectives—objectives antithetical to yours and your children's. It's your job to secure the right lawyer, one who will represent your concerns and those of your children before his own. To find the right attorney, you must first understand what many lawyers care about in custody battles.

• THE LAWYER'S INTERESTS ARE NOT NECESSARILY • YOUR INTERESTS

You must keep in mind, above all, that you and your former husband have the health, well-being, and future of your children at stake. You may also have some property issues to work out. Many lawyers, unfortunately, have one overriding interest: their fees. You might argue that they also have their reputations at stake, but as one lawyer informed me, reputation is not nearly as important as you might think, especially if you live in a big city. "If you practice in a big city," this attorney told me, "you're always going to have clients, because the city itself is too big for word to spread, and of course the population is changing and usually growing. Unless you create a scandal that appears in the newspapers and on television, your business is pretty safe."

Obviously, it is in the best interests of your children, you, and your former husband to resolve your case quickly, preferably within thirty to sixty days. However, there is a very real temptation for lawyers to extend your case for as long as possible, for the simple reason that they make more money the longer your case runs. Lawyers can extend a case in a variety of ways, and they can do so with complete impunity.

Ironically, you can even abet them in their efforts if you do not understand the many behaviors that you, your husband, and the lawyers can engage in that will protract your custody battle. You should never lose sight of the fact that the longer the battle goes on, the greater the pain caused to your children, to you, and to your former husband.

I am not mentioning your former husband out of altruism. I do so only to be realistic. The more upset both of you become with each other, the more vulnerable you are to self-destructive emotions and behavior, especially anger and revenge. As the emotions become more intense, as the stakes get higher, and as the demands become more intractable, the length of the proceedings will extend. Meanwhile, the human and financial costs will increase and it will become increasingly difficult to reach a settlement out of court.

• HOW LAWYERS CHURN A CUSTODY CASE •

By their very nature, custody cases are adversarial situations, meaning that one parent is pitted against the other. Both people have already failed at working out a life together, which is why they are divorced and embroiled in a custody battle. This means that they have negative and often hostile feelings about each other sitting just below the surface, waiting to emerge. All your lawyer has to do is go to your former husband's attorney and make a lot of outrageous demands in order for the underlying feelings to surface. Your former husband's attorney then comes back with a set of equally exaggerated counterdemands, which anger and terrify you. Now you have a lot of emotion to resolve before the two of you can start talking sanely to each other. Meanwhile, the two attorneys can make matters even worse by taking additional depositions from you and your former husband. Those depositions often make both of you mad and entrench you even more deeply in your respective demands, making compromise all the more difficult to reach. In effect, the process actually drives the two parents further apart. With the encouragement of both lawyers, you and your former husband are now building a wall between the two of you, a wall that ultimately will come down on one or both of your heads—and the heads of your children.

I am reminded of one of those street fights in which the two combatants are being egged on by their so-called friends. In the legal profession, such behavior is referred to as churning a case, meaning that both lawyers stir the emotional pot just enough to get the two parties angry at each other. It is done every day in tens of thousands of cases. The lawyers, of course, are protected from any accusations from you, because they can argue that their opening gambit was merely a negotiating strategy designed to get the most for their clients. In fact, that strategy, either inadvertently or by design, inflames the emotions, polarizes the parents, and extends the process. Meanwhile, the lawyers are billing you for outrageous sums of money for every minute they even consider your name.

But higher legal fees are not the only cost. As compromise and settlement become more and more unlikely, the situation becomes more and more complicated and destructive. Ultimately, of course, you will wind up in court, where things can really get ugly.

The courts are overcrowded, which often means that your case may not be heard for at least six to nine months. Very often the case may not get to court for more than a year, perhaps two. (My own case took eighteen months before a judge made a decision.)

However, long before you get to court, there will be more depositions, interrogatories, and investigations into your life, your children's lives, and your former husband's life by court-appointed psychotherapists and human resource personnel. As I will explain in greater detail later in this book, these people will evaluate every detail of your life and the lives of your children. These investigations are not only disruptive but often personally injurious.

As the proceedings drag on, emotions become frayed, hostilities increase, and demands become more intractable. The level of stress becomes unbearable—not just for you but for your children.

At some point, the court may appoint a guardian ad litem, which is an attorney who will represent your children. If the court appoints such an attorney, you will have no choice but to hire that person, at your and your former husband's expense. The cost of such a lawyer can range from several hundred to several thousand dollars. The purpose of the guardian ad litem is to represent your children's interests. This attorney will sit down with your children and ask them about their lives, their present living arrangements, and whom they want to live with after the proceedings conclude. The lawyer will also determine if the children have any special need for legal representation. Their answers may have an impact on the judge's decision, but they are rarely decisive. The judge will decide whom the children will live with on a much wider range of evidence. Ironically, the guardian ad litem may not render any specific service to your children at all. Many parents get a letter and perhaps a phone call telling them that a guardian ad litem has been appointed, but that may be all they ever hear from such a person.

My own experience is that the guardian ad litem is a costly and useless appendage to the process. In the end, the guardian ad litem will do little or nothing for your children except add to their stress and your own. The attorney will merely complicate matters, being just another person to place in your schedule and to make sure your children meet, if in fact he or she deigns to meet your children at all. And after the suit is over, the lawyer presents you with a significant legal bill. In my case, the guardian ad litem actually slowed down and complicated the process, making it more costly in every way for all of us.

Still, the demands placed on you mean nothing to many lawyers. Their ultimate goal is to move the process all the way to a court hearing and a judge's decision because that's the point at which the legal costs will have reached their maximum.

Many women find themselves in situations in which their lawyers are churning their cases. Attorneys are able to do this because they know the women they represent are terrified of losing their children and will do almost anything to keep that from happening. They have their clients over a barrel and they know just how to work the system to achieve maximum benefit—for themselves!

Women inadvertently fall into the lawyer's trap by thinking that they must be tough with their former husband, especially at the outset of their negotiating process. Being tough translates for many women into being intractable and angry. What women forget is that the more intransigent they become, the higher the financial and emotional toll is to themselves and their children. Certainly it takes two to reach a settlement. And former husbands are usually just as intractable, if not more so. After all, they are usually the ones that initiate the lawsuit. So there's good reason to be angry, hurt, and demanding. There's also a natural desire for revenge. But there's a big difference between having those feelings and basing your strategy upon them. If you have an attorney who wants to churn your case, he or she will play on those emotions, which will only make matters more complicated, expensive, and painful.

My purpose in this chapter is to help you avoid that situation. Here's how you can do it.

• FINDING THE RIGHT LAWYER •

The best place to start in your search for the right lawyer is by asking friends, business associates, a family doctor, clergy, or other lawyers for a referral. Ask people you trust and respect. Do not hire someone who is shouting the loudest on television or in the yellow pages. Very often these people are more hype than substance. At the very least, you do not know what you are getting. Remember, your children are on the line here. Try to avoid hiring someone who doesn't come highly recommended.

Places to look for a lawyer, especially if you are concerned about costs—and who isn't?—include the following:

- Local legal aid societies
- County courthouses and their "lawyer of the day" programs
- Battered women's shelters
- Mediation programs and counselors

There is a reference available in most libraries called the *Martindale Hubbell Law Directory* that rates attorneys. A lawyer with an A rating is considered preeminently qualified; B is eminently qualified; C is qualified. Each state's bar association reports any disciplinary actions taken against an attorney, but these reports—or the lack of them—are a poor guide, since even bad lawyers usually avoid disciplinary action by local bar associations.

In general, you want someone with a quiet, understated competence. You do not want anyone who is attempting to make a name for himself by trying your case in the newspapers. For the same reason, you do not want a high-profile attorney, one who by his very nature attracts attention. A child custody suit can be among the most humiliating experiences you will ever undergo. You want to hire someone who is sensitive and discreet, who can keep your experience private, and who is able to support you as you go through a very trying time.

Do not hire a friend unless your friend happens to be the best family attorney in the country—and even then think twice. Never choose a lawyer who is a friend of your husband. He or she will be compromised from the start. If you have a friend who is a lawyer, ask him or her for a referral.

You want to hire the best and most competent attorney that you can afford. You are about to be thrown into the lion's den. Hire a person who has been there before and has come away from the ordeal with the client's children safely in hand. You should not hire anyone exclusively on the basis of sex, race, ethnic background, or religion. Be very clear with yourself that such factors mean nothing when it comes to a person's competence. However, you should ask yourself whether you feel more comfortable talking to a woman than to a man, or to someone of the same ethnic origin, race, or religious affiliation. I ask you to consider these factors only because you need to talk openly and honestly to this person and because communication is second only to competence. If you feel that you can talk more openly with a woman, or with a man for that matter, then let that be one of many factors that you consider in deciding which attorney will represent you.

Keep in mind that if you do have to go to court, you will be judged in part by your lawyer's manner, appearance, and appeal (or the lack of it). A feminist with a chip on her shoulder or a loud, outspoken man will not serve your purposes in a courtroom.

• CAN YOU COMMUNICATE WITH THIS PERSON? •

Before hiring an attorney, you will want to sit down with him or her to discuss your case. Most lawyers will grant an initial interview for free. It is not a good sign if a lawyer charges you an exorbitant fee for an initial interview. It suggests that the fee is everything and may reveal a character who might be tempted to churn your case. No matter whom you choose, try to select someone who radiates maturity, stability, and wisdom. You want someone to represent *your* values and beliefs.

Here are some questions you want to ask a prospective attorney early in the interview.

How long have you been practicing and how many custody cases have you handled?

Though there is no real cutoff point in terms of years in practice, you want someone who is experienced. The person should not be fresh out of law school and using your case to learn his or her trade. In Dade County, Florida, there were more than 15,000 new lawyers admitted to the bar during the last decade or so. No doubt some very young attorneys are handling child custody cases. Don't let one of them be yours.

How will you keep me informed as the case evolves? May I telephone you with questions, or do you turn me over to staff for most queries? Do you return calls promptly?

The lawyer should assure you that her staff will not be used as a buffer between her and you. Much of your communication will be by letter, but whenever something occurs that needs your immediate attention, or when there is an event in the case that you should know about it, your lawyer should telephone you herself. If it's a fairly routine matter and she can't call you, she should have a staff member call. She should then follow up that call with one of her own. If it's a sensitive matter, she should call you herself. You should be able to call your attorney with any questions you may have. You don't want to engage your lawyer with questions that can be answered by her staff or that don't need her immediate attention. For one thing, it's costly; for another, it places a burden on the attorney. Eventually you can be seen as a troublesome client, which in all too many cases results in higher legal costs (about which, more later).

Can you provide at least half a dozen referrals from former clients?

Follow up your interview by telephoning former clients who have been represented by your prospective attorney. Ask them about their experiences with the lawyer in question. Among the most important questions you want to ask is whether the lawyer was successful at gaining custody of the woman's children for her, and whether the attorney did all he or she could to settle the case before going to court. These are the key questions. Above all else, you want to win custody or custodial care of your children; you want the proceedings to be handled as quickly as possible; and you want to keep costs down. Ask how much the case cost the former client and whether the attorney was agreeable to negotiating his or her fee. (More on this below.) Property issues will very likely figure in your concerns as well. Ask any questions you may have about these areas, but do not lose sight of your main priorities. You want to win custody of your children and you want to do it as expeditiously as possible.

Do you have malpractice insurance?

About 10 percent of lawyers do, and usually it's the very competent people who have it. You obviously don't want to enter a relationship with an attorney thinking that you may have to sue him or her after this process is over, but as one lawyer who has such insurance told me, "If I screw up, at least there's something there that people can come back at me for."

During your initial interview with your attorney, you must ask at least some of the questions I have suggested. They are the basis for establishing an honest relationship with someone who will be of vital importance to you over the next few months or years. There is no way to overestimate the importance of this relationship. This person has to be able to walk through hell with you. And you'll have to be able to share very personal and sensitive information with him or her (see Chapter 3).

As you ask your questions, listen carefully to see if the attorney answers them clearly and honestly. Does he explain himself adequately? Does she communicate understanding, tolerance, and patience, or is she rushing you through the interview? How do you feel about this person? Could you discuss with him or her all the very personal issues that will come up during the proceedings? Ask yourself: Is this the person that I should be working with?

For the initial interview, these opening questions should give you enough information to decide if you want to hire this person. Before you make such a decision, however, you will have to know what the attorney will charge you to handle your case. At this initial interview, therefore, you should discuss the lawyer's fee.

• THE COSTS •

Unless you find a lawyer who will take your case on a low-fee basis, your legal costs will likely range between $15,000 and $20,000—at the minimum. Please be aware that these figures are very soft. A lot depends on the lawyer's strategy, his or her capacity to find a middle ground with your former husband, and your former husband's willingness to compromise. A lawyer will quote you an hourly rate that will range from $150 to $450 an hour. Needless to say, the longer your case goes on, the more it will cost you. It is not uncommon for people to spend $75,000 to $100,000 on a child custody suit. Such amounts are referred to by ethical lawyers as obscene, yet they are common. As one Florida lawyer told me, "Attorneys are funding their Fisher Island lifestyle on the tears of children," referring to the upscale resort off the South Florida coast. You will want to do all you can to limit costs.

You can begin to limit costs simply by telling your prospective attorney what you can afford. Give him or her specific instructions. An attorney told me recently that "a lawyer should be told how much money you want to spend. Don't give him or her carte blanche. Tell him that this is all the money you have and you cannot spend any more than this."

Discuss the costs of everything, including the attorney's hourly fee, copying costs, billing for telephone calls, and whether you are billed portal to portal, meaning from the moment the attorney leaves the office to the time he or she arrives at court or whatever destination he or she is going to on your behalf. Traffic can be very costly. A one-hour meeting can turn out to be three hours in billing fees.

Try to negotiate the hourly rate. Tell him or her that you cannot afford to pay $150 an hour and ask if the rate can be reduced at all. Ask if the attorney can waive the charges for photocopies of documents. Ask if you can reduce the costs by performing any copying or other services for which you would otherwise be billed. Remember this: Everything is negotiable and a discussion about every billed item is appropriate, especially at the outset of your relationship. Whatever you do, do not act overly submissive or naive when it comes to money. It's like going to a plastic surgeon and saying "Make me beautiful." The cash register just starts ringing.

Ask the lawyer to give you a written contract spelling out his or her hourly fee, all the related costs, what he or she agrees to do for the fee, and the limit he or she can bill you. Without such a retainer, your attorney has a free hand to spend as much of your money as he or she sees fit.

Certain documents you can obtain yourself and furnish to your attorney and thereby save some money. Some of these documents will be in your possession; others are part of the public record and can be obtained at your local county tax registry, bureau of deeds, or town hall. Among them are:

- Marriage certificate
- Divorce decree
- Any documents from prior divorce proceedings
- Tax returns
- Mortgages
- Deeds
- Insurance policies
- Bank statements
- Wills
- Pension handbook

• DON'T CHANGE LAWYERS •

Once you find a lawyer you feel you can work with, then commit yourself to her or him. Don't waver in your commitment and don't change lawyers. It's highly disruptive—you have to start the entire process all over again—and expensive. I know; I had to do both.

When I was first served the child custody papers by my former husband, I immediately ran out and hired a lawyer who was a longtime friend of mine (my first mistake). After looking over the facts in the case, his first words to me were "Don't worry, he [my former husband] doesn't stand a chance. We'll have this whole thing straightened out in no time." Certainly from all outward appearances I appeared to be in a much better position to raise our children than my former husband. I had a successful therapy practice; I was making an excellent living; and I had very flexible hours that allowed me to be with my children.

Still, I nearly lost my custody case. My former husband hired a skilled lawyer committed to stretching out the process. Once the process was extended, a plethora of experts was called in to evaluate me, my former husband, and our children. As time dragged on, the case became increasingly complicated. Eventually my attorney-friend realized he was way out of his depth and that we were facing a real battle. We parted company and I was forced to start over with a new attorney. It was a year and a half before a judgment was finally rendered.

These questions and issues are all part of your preliminary discussion, however. After you are satisfied with the person's competence, reputation, manner, and track record, and after you have settled all the costs to your satisfaction, you will want to discuss his or her philosophy and approach to your case.

• THE KEY: HIS OR HER APPROACH TO SETTLEMENT •

The most important question you can ask a prospective attorney is what his or her attitude is toward settling your case before it reaches court. Your attorney's strategy should be designed to arrive at a successful settlement with your former husband so that you retain custody of your children and avoid going to court.

One attorney put it this way: "When a client hires me, I tell her or him that it is my philosophy and intention to resolve this matter before going to court. It's better for both parents and better for the children. There's less time involved, less money, and less heartache. We have to do all we can to resolve this conflict as quickly as possible."

As I mentioned in the Introduction, a child custody suit may occur at the time of divorce or well after a divorce occurs. If the suit occurs as part of a divorce, there will be numerous property issues to be settled, in addition to the custody issues. However, even if the custody case arises well after the divorce has occurred, it's very common for old property disputes to arise again as part of the custody battle.

Among the issues you and your former husband may be confronting are the following:

- Custodial rights of the children, or the question of where they will live on a full-time basis. (This includes the type of custody that you and your former husband are fighting over. More on the various kinds of custody rights below.)
- Visitation rights. These vary depending on how far apart the parents live from each other. Common questions to be resolved are: Will the children visit the noncustodial parent every other weekend? Will they be allowed to stay over Sunday night and brought to school by the noncustodial parent on Monday morning? Will the children be allowed to visit the noncustodial parent during the middle of the week? Where will the children stay on birthdays and major holidays? Will holidays be divided between the two of you, so that you have them on some holidays while their father has them on others? How long can the children go away on vacations with the noncustodial parent? How frequent can those vacations be?
- Relocation rights. Can the custodial parent relocate the children to another state or a distant part of the country? Often, there are restrictions on how far away the children can be

moved from the noncustodial parent without the noncustodial parent's permission. In most cases, these will be determined by the court. If you want to relocate after the court has made its decision, you will most likely need a judge to grant permission for such a move.

• The amount of child support you will receive. Typically, child support is figured on a formula outlined in the statutes of most states. As a general rule of thumb, a woman with one child will receive roughly the equivalent of one week's salary from her husband per month. If she has two children, she will receive approximately one-third of his monthly income per month. The formula allows for increases in the amount of child support for women with more than two children. A ceiling has been set at 60 percent of the husband's disposable income—that is, after taxes and essential expenses have been taken out of his monthly salary.

Very important: You will have to discuss exactly how much child support you will need very early in your relationship with your attorney. In fact, once you hire your attorney, that will be one of the first items of business—establishing how much support you will need from your former husband each month. In Chapter 3, I discuss how essential it is to keep a log of monthly expenses and how such a log forms the foundation for your claims for child support.

• Alimony, if any. Will you receive alimony payments, or if you were the primary breadwinner, will he receive any alimony?

• Ownership of the family's former home. Also, who will live in the family house, if anyone? Will it be sold? If so, how will the funds be divided?

• Ownership of other valuable property, including stocks and bonds, cars, furniture, appliances, a second home, a boat. If that property is sold, how will the proceeds be divided?

• Ownership of a family business. If the company was jointly owned, will the former partner retain ownership of his or her share of the business or be bought out? If a buyout occurs, how much will the spouse receive for his or her shares of the business?

Your attorney should identify the items you are utterly committed to and those on which you are flexible. She should tell you that you will not get everything you want; on some of the issues, you'll have to compromise. That's the only way a negotiation can come to a satisfactory conclusion. Custody is not one of those issues, however. You must be absolutely adamant that you receive custody or custodial care of the children. On the other hand, there may be other issues—such as child support— that you must also be committed to. Be clear about every one of your demands. Separate the items you insist on from those you will be flexible about so that your attorney can develop a clear negotiating strategy.

As one lawyer told me, "There may be ten issues at stake in a custody battle. Maybe there are three or four that are absolutely sacred; the others can be negotiated. I find out what the parameters are or how flexible my client can be. I then structure a settlement resolution and start the negotiating process." After your attorney knows where you stand, he or she will set a settlement conference with your former husband's attorney.

Your attorney should attempt to separate the custody and visitation issues from the property disputes. This should be one of the ground rules of the negotiating process. Very often, children are used as pawns to get money or ownership of property. Many a woman tells a former husband that if he grants her custodial care of the children, she will give up her rights to the house and other property. Husbands say, if you give me liberal visitation rights, I'll grant you this much in child support. This is wrong and often the basis for one or the other parent to sue for custody again later on. Women are entitled to child support and 50 percent of the ownership of property. A good attorney will spell out the law and insist you get all you need and deserve to support your children and yourself in the wake of your settlement or court-mandated arrangement.

• DON'T MAKE IT HARD FOR YOURSELF •

While you make your demands, however, you must not inject revenge into this process. This only complicates the negotiating process and makes it more difficult to reach a settlement. So many parents want to settle old scores with their former spouse that they lose sight of the big picture, the real purpose of the negotiating process. They become unreasonable in their demands as a way to hurt their former spouse. Many women argue that their former husbands are poor fathers or bad men, and therefore they're not going to give them liberal visitation rights. Lawyers tell me all the time that women come right out and say to them, "He's not paying me adequate child support," or "He regularly misses child support payments, so I'm going to limit his visitation rights." Many women admit to their attorneys that they want to turn their former husband's life into a "nightmare. I want to limit his visitation, and every time he sets foot in my house, I'm going to make it hell for him."

Many men and women incorrectly believe that if they go to court, they will somehow be exonerated by the judge, who will condemn the other spouse for his or her behavior over the years. The judge will thus be their instrument of revenge. This belief makes such a hearing appealing to many people. Allow me to dispel this fantasy. The judge is not going to exonerate anyone. Most judges remain absolutely objective and eventually make their ruling as coolly as possible. However, judges who do comment on the case at hand usually scold both parents. In fact, by the time the hearing ends, you will have been evaluated, judged, and written about by so many people—including psychologists, human resource people, and the judge himself—that you will both wish you had never gone that far.

Attorneys report that when their clients are clearheaded, have their emotions under control, know what they need, and are willing to be flexible, they can come away with an expeditious settlement and get most of what they wanted.

Decide where you must stand firm and where you can compromise. Such an approach is the basis for a successful negotiating strategy.

Once your attorney has a clear picture of your priorities, he or she must communicate to your husband's lawyer that you are flexible and willing to compromise. It's also important to let your former husband and his attorney know that you wish to settle things amicably and to avoid going to court. Your attorney can even spell out your reasons for avoiding a court battle, the most important of which is to protect your children from the terrible consequences of such a fight.

The two attorneys will discuss the points under dispute and attempt to establish common ground for a settlement. This may take numerous conversations between the attorneys, who will relay all the information to you and your former husband. The two of you then make your counteroffers and, it is hoped, inch closer to each other. As you draw nearer to a settlement, your lawyer may suggest that a conference occur, in which you, your former husband, and your respective lawyers meet to finalize an agreement.

Depending on the feelings between you and your former husband, you and he may or may not be present in the room while that conference is taking place. If there is a great deal of animosity between the two of you, your lawyers should meet in a separate room and try to hammer out a settlement. One lawyer told me that he takes a partially prepared agreement into the conference and then negotiates the rest of the agreement with the spouse's attorney. Once an oral agreement has been reached, the two attorneys will get your and your former husband's signature on the document immediately. Unlike a settlement reached through a mediator, this agreement is legally binding once it is signed.

If negotiation fails and a settlement cannot be reached, you will have to hunker down and prepare for a hearing with a judge. You'll have to stay in close contact with your attorney, as well as with her staff.

It's a good idea to cultivate good relations with your attorney's staff, including legal assistants and secretaries. They help your lawyer put your case together and play a vital role in your entire case. Also, you will be talking to these people almost daily, asking for information and passing your thoughts on to your lawyer. They can be your allies or your enemies. Everyone who works in your lawyer's office will contribute to the way in which you are seen. That attitude can filter upward and even make its way into court, to the very people who will be deciding your fate.

• QUESTIONS TO ASK YOUR LAWYER ABOUT CUSTODY •

Here are some of the additional questions you will want to ask your attorney. I have provided general answers to give you some background before you consult your attorney.

What is the difference between various types of custodies, such as joint, residential, and sole legal custody?

The definitions vary somewhat from state to state. However, in general, *sole legal custody*, often referred to simply as legal custody, means that one parent alone is responsible for all the decisions concerning the children's lives. Obviously, the children also live with that parent.

Many states refer to *joint legal custody*, which means that both parents share responsibility equally for all decisions concerning their children, such as medical and dental care, education, religious training, discipline, and social life. *Joint physical custody* means that the child spends relatively equal amounts of time in each parent's home. In other words, the two parents share physical custody of the children equally.

Physical custody, or custodial care or custodial rights, means that one parent provides the primary residence or home for the children and has day-to-day responsibility for the children's lives.

Bird's nest custody is a form of joint custody in which the children remain in the home and the parents take turns moving in and out of the home.

How much of a say do my children have in who they want to live with?

A judge will take into account the preferences of the children, but it is only one of many factors taken into account in making his or her final decision. The children will not have a unilateral say in where they live or with whom, however. (See Chapter 3 for more on how the judge will decide your case.)

What are the different kinds of visitation rights that courts impose?

There are generally three types of visitation rights. The first is called *reasonable* or *flexible* visitation, which means the court leaves it to the parents to work out the times and places that the noncustodial parent will visit the children or the children will visit the noncustodial parent. In this case, there must be a great deal of interaction and cooperation between the parents, since they will have to work out on a regular basis when, where, and how the children will get together with the noncustodial parent.

Fixed visitation establishes a fixed schedule for the children to see their noncustodial parent, such as Tuesdays and Thursdays and every other weekend, for example. This schedule is often imposed on the parents by the court when the two have hostile feelings toward each other. The fixed schedule requires far less interaction between the parents and is court imposed, which means the schedule must be abided to.

Supervised visitation involves the noncustodial parent's seeing the children in the presence of another adult, usually someone other than the custodial parent. The adult supervisor may be someone agreed upon by the parents or appointed by the court. However, no matter who it is, the person must be approved by the court.

What are typical visitation arrangements with a noncustodial parent?

Usually, parents agree to have the children spend alternate weekends with the noncustodial parent and regular three-day holidays. Parents will have to decide whether or not to allow midweek visitations, and if so, how the children will get to school the following day. Children usually spend part of their summer vacations with their noncustodial parent, along with winter or spring breaks. Often they alternate every other year with their noncustodial parent during major holidays, such as Thanksgiving, Christmas, Hanukkah, Passover, and Easter. Birthdays and key family anniversaries are often negotiated in the same way.

How can the children be protected from a parent who has been physically or sexually abusive to the children?

If physical or sexual abuse is proved, the court will prevent the abusive parent from having any form of custody. The court will likely require that the parent undergo some type of counseling; in fact, in cases of sexual abuse or extreme physical abuse, the destructive adult may face criminal charges and imprisonment. At the very least, the court will require supervised visitation.

Can I stop visitation by my former husband if he stops or suspends his child support payments?

No. If child support payments are stopped, however, your lawyer should file a contempt action to enforce the court's order for support.

Can visitation be denied?

Yes, but only under certain very specific conditions, such as proven physical abuse, neglect, or exposure of the children to dangerous situations or drug or alcohol abuse. As I describe at length in Chapter 3, the fate of your children will be decided according to what the court decides is in their best interests. Judges believe correctly that it is in the best interests of the children for them to see both parents. Only under extreme and proven conditions, such as those described above, will a court deny a parent visitation rights. In most cases, a judge will order that visitation be supervised before preventing it altogether.

If my former husband and I share custody of our children, does that mean I don't get child support payments?

You will get child support, but it may be reduced if joint or shared custody is ordered.

At what age will my children stop receiving child support?

Again, it varies from state to state, but many states have mandated that child support will continue up to the time that a child graduates from college or reaches the ages of twenty-three.

Will the court allow me to relocate and take my children with me?

In many cases, yes, but you will have to request permission from the court, especially if you are moving a substantial distance from your current location. When considering whether a parent has the right to relocate, the court takes into account several key factors, among them: whether your material conditions and those of your children will be enhanced by the move; what effect the move will have on the existing visitation agreement with your former spouse; the emotional, psychological, academic, and religious ties your children may have to their current community; and finally, the children's concerns and desires regarding the move. You will have to formally petition the court to relocate, and all of these factors will be considered at length by the judge before he or she decides whether to give you permission to make your move.

Once you have agreed to be represented by a particular attorney, don't waste your money and your attorney's time by asking him or her to give you psychological support whenever you're feeling down or depressed. Unnecessary telephone time sends the legal fees skyrocketing. Don't call your attorney with every question that comes to mind. Instead, make a list of questions and then ask them in a single telephone call. If the subject requires that you speak to your attorney in private, schedule a meeting. Be thorough, get all your questions and concerns addressed, but use your time and money efficiently. Don't meet with your attorney unless there are certain questions that only he or she can answer.

Your attorney is your skilled advocate and guide through these terrible waters. But you still must do a lot on your own to build a solid case. That's your next step: giving your attorney the ammunition he or she needs to fight and win this battle.

2 THE MYTH OF THE GOOD MOTHER

After you have hired a lawyer, the real work begins: proving yourself to be the most appropriate parent to take custodial care of your children. This is not a job that you simply turn over to your attorney. Only you can prove your fitness as a parent. The first step in doing that is to approach the fight that you face correctly. I say that because the job of proving yourself to be a good mother is fraught with mental and emotional pitfalls. The very act of attempting to prove such a thing brings up all sorts of doubts, especially for working mothers, who already suffer from guilt. In your case, however, it's far worse because your former husband and his lawyers will do all they can to prove that you are an unfit parent.

That very struggle—on the one hand, your efforts to prove your fitness, and on the other, the accusations by your husband that you were anything but—may eventually become internalized by you until you are at war with yourself. You are at once your own prosecutor and your own defender. You attack yourself for not doing this or that, but then you enter into long monologues about how you are doing this or that for your children. It's a long internal debate, or rather a war. And it can be exhausting. The accusations eat away at you. They can erode your confidence and belief in yourself until you are overwhelmed with guilt, anger, even rage. Over time, you appreciate less and less about yourself as a mother, even as you fight to retain custody of your children.

What is really happening? we should ask ourselves. In fact,

you, your husband, his lawyer, and eventually the judge are dealing with a myth, the myth of the perfect mother.

That image of the perfect mother is the invisible presence in every child custody suit. The image looms behind you like a giant shadow. You, the working mother, will be compared with and judged by your resemblance to this image. You have loved your children with all the love you have. You have sacrificed your own desires, pleasures, time, and energy for their sake, and you don't regret it. Yet your former husband and his lawyers will try to convince a judge that you were never a mother in anything but the biological sense, that you neglected your children or that you were mentally unstable or that your former husband was always the better parent.

Make no mistake: You, the mother, are the one on trial here. Very few fathers can win a custody battle against a woman who is demonstrably a good mother. The court would rather give custodial care of the children to their mother than to their father *unless the mother is proven an unworthy parent.* In that case, all the father has to be is adequate and he will get the children. Therefore, the primary strategy of the father and his attorney will be to impeach you as an unworthy mother. You are under suspicion from the very beginning, especially if you are a working mother. Your former husband's strategy will be to dismiss all the acts of mothering that you performed for your children. Don't you join him in that denial.

If you are like most working mothers today, you may be a little guilt-ridden over your role as a mother. In fact, mothers are so filled with guilt that they can very easily accept and participate in dismissing all the love and sacrifice they have given as mothers. The guilt we may feel can cause us to believe that we are failures at life's most important role. In a child custody case, there is no room for failure. If you present yourself as a mother who has fallen short of the mythical image of the perfect mother, you can lose your children. Therefore, one of the essential steps in winning your custody suit is honoring yourself as a mother and then *presenting yourself* as a mother to be honored—not only by your children, but by the judge who will determine their fate and yours.

To do that, you must understand two things very intimately. First, you must better understand this image of the perfect mother. Second, you must see your job as mother in a new, more realistic context, free of the burden of comparison with the image of the perfect mother. Let's have a look at both the myth and the reality of motherhood.

• THE ARCHETYPE OF THE GREAT MOTHER •

The image of the perfect mother exists in our consciousness and, to a greater extent, our unconscious as an archetype, much like the image of the perfect father or hero or saint. The image of the archetypal mother has existed in virtually every culture in human history as a goddess figure. Perhaps her earliest appearance occurred in Greece as Gaia, the Mother Earth. According to Greek mythology, Gaia preceded all other immortals and gave birth to other gods. The Great Mother was known as Ceres to the ancient Romans, Artemis in Ephesus, Inanna-Ishtar in Mesopotamia, the Goddess Nut to the ancient Egyptians, and later in Egypt as Isis. She was the Earth Woman to the Navajo, the Corn Mother to other Native Americans, including the Hopi, Izanami to the Japanese, and Quan Yin to the Chinese. Of course, the Great Mother figure Christians are most aware of is Mary, the mother of Jesus. Interestingly, Jesus is accompanied by two mother figures—Mary, his mother, and Mary Magdalene, a prostitute who falls in love with him and becomes his follower. Both are healers, but in different ways. Both demonstrate commitment and sacrifice, characteristics common to the mother image.

Among the characteristics almost universally ascribed to the Great Mother is the capacity to give birth, heal the sick, and restore the dead to life. She protects her children, watches over the dead—or the sleeping, as the dead are often referred to mythologically—and eventually gives them new life. As such, she is the source of rebirth and even forgiveness. These characteristics are much in demand today, of course, especially from men, who unconsciously ask women to create miracles in their lives, to compensate them for their wounds, and ultimately to grant them rebirth. In any case, the archetypal mother image in virtually all cultures, including our own, is a divine personage, a goddess.

Traditionally, the Great Mother possessed a wide range of paradoxical emotions and characteristics. Just as she could be all loving, she could also at times be harsh and punitive. Gradually, over the last two thousand years, Mary has emerged as an evolutionary step in the archetypal mother image. According to Christian tradition, Mary, who is free of all evil, is the source of unconditional love. As such, she is beyond all dualities, such as light and dark, love and hatred, joy and fear. Her love is unconditional, meaning it goes out to all people, regardless of religious background, past behavior, or any misdeed they may have committed. Such is the nature of unconditional love: There is no way you can exist outside its embrace.

The capacity to give unconditional love is wholly within the domain of the archetypal mother, no matter what form she may take. The Great Mother need not be Mary per se but any goddess figure who represents the ideals of motherhood. Tall and thin, short and robust, black, white, or yellow, the Great Mother has now emerged in human consciousness as the source of unconditional love in the universe. Some argue that unconditional love would not even exist as a thought or an unreachable ideal were it not for the presence of the archetypal mother in the human psyche.

As with many other mythical images that live within us, the image of the Great Mother serves as a source of strength and inspiration, rather than as actual standards for judging human behavior. This image is there to guide us toward a higher way of living; it serves as our lodestar on our journey through life. In the end, the image of the Great Mother spurs us toward a greater capacity to love, including a greater capacity to love ourselves.

The image of the Great Mother is not to be confused with being human. As humans we live in the world of duality—of good and evil, day and night, light and dark—and are therefore paradoxical in nature. We are composed of strengths and weaknesses, love and hate, joy and fear, forgiveness and rigidity. We all possess characteristics and talents. We also bear within us so many darker conditions, including anger, jealousy, and the desire for revenge. We are composed of opposites. None of us is all good or all evil; we are both, striving to enlarge the good.

We also are wounded human beings in need of healing. To heal means to become whole. To be whole means to become unified, singular, or integrated. The act of integration is actually the job of rescuing parts of ourselves from our own self-criticism and negative judgment. Repressed memories, humiliating or shameful experiences, unwanted characteristics—all these must be restored to love if we are to be integrated and whole human beings. We must love ourselves for all our parts if we are to be healed.

Since, as we said, humanity exists in the world of duality, we are not yet fully integrated, we are not yet whole.

The archetype of the Great Mother is whole, unified, and fully integrated. This is what has made her worthy of a world beyond duality and paradox—the unified world where all is love. Her status as a singular oneness gives her the capacity for unconditional love. Unlike the archetypal father, who sets standards for behavior, out of which come laws of conduct, the archetypal mother loves unceasingly and without conditions.

Mothers—that is, ordinary human women—have always been the only human beings capable of coming close to that archetypal ideal. True, all mothers love their children conditionally—

ultimately, we fail at unconditional love—but if any expression gets close to the ideal, it is the love a mother has for her child. It is for this reason, many believe, that mothers don't make wars; nor are we the perpetrators of most of the violence, in part because we know that every human being is some mother's child. Instead, we heal the wounded, we soothe the suffering, we forgive the misdeeds of others.

• COUNTERFEIT IMAGES AND REAL LIFE •

After World War II, when so many families lost loved ones in the war and so many men returned home wounded and broken, American society was in need of healing and forgiveness. Naturally, the nation turned to the archetypal mother for solace. At the end of the war, women went from the factories—where they served the nation while the men were away—to the home, where they restored and healed the wounded American family. The image of the perfect woman was suddenly the perfect mother, explicitly selfless, implicitly a magical healer.

Our society began turning out derivative images of the archetypal mother, especially in the media. One of the main purveyors of that image, of course, was television, especially during the 1950s and '60s. Such shows as *Ozzie and Harriet*, *Father Knows Best*, *Leave It to Beaver*, and *The Donna Reed Show* depicted a suburban heaven in which Mother ruled the home while Father ruled the world. The versions of the perfect mother that appeared on these shows were no more real than the images of American society, or of the perfect father, for that matter. These were fiction. Remarkably, while men weren't held to the standards of the perfect father—that is, financially successful, temperamentally balanced, and downright Solomon-like in judgment—the women were expected to be every bit the equal of these perfect females. Interestingly, in the last decade or so, television all but abandoned family life and instead chose to give us sitcoms about single men and women, most of whom are in their twenties and thirties, who are engaged primarily in sexual situations. Sex and physical beauty have overshadowed the problems of families as the source of most entertainment. The net effect of this turning away from the family, however, was that we were left with all of those old images of the perfect mother that have never been updated. Women still talk about being compared to images that stopped being relevant twenty-five years ago.

But let's have a closer look at these mythical women to see if there is any real basis for comparison to real life. The fictional perfect mother, as portrayed by American media, has the following lifestyle and characteristics:

The fictional mother lives in a suburban heaven that is inherently safe, orderly, and intimate.
People know each other well; they are friends and support one another; and the antagonists are really well meaning at heart.

I raised my children in Miami, Florida, a big city known for, among other things, its high crime rate, drug abuse, violence, and urban sprawl. My children attended public schools in Miami, where they were as much concerned about violence as they were about their grades. Drugs are prevalent throughout the school system today and influence school life in countless ways, all of them detrimental to the health and well-being of families. The burdens placed on families today by the problems of the city, suburbia, and the modern school system are more than the perfect mother ever dreamed of.

The fictional mother has her financial needs met by her husband and therefore does not need to work outside her home.
Today, 70 percent of mothers with children under twelve years of age work outside the home. The primary reason women work is that families cannot afford the American lifestyle without two

incomes. The cost of housing, transportation, food, clothing, and other necessities cannot be met by the income provided by most men today. Consequently, women must work if we are to meet the financial demands of our times. I was among those working women. I considered myself fortunate because I could schedule my clients around many of my children's major events. I could also be home occasionally when they returned from school. But I missed a lot of their lives for the simple reason that I had to work to earn a living.

The fictional mother has time.

She spends hours in the kitchen, where she turns out spectacular meals and an endless supply of cookies, and then before her mirror, where she dresses and makes herself up to be a glowing beauty. Like most real mothers, I spend my day running from one appointment to the next. I shuttle my children to various sporting events and extracurricular activities and take them on shopping expeditions. I wedge these trips between my work appointments. In short, I spend most of my adult life stressed and harried. I don't have a lot of time to spend in front of the mirror, though I have made it a priority to take care of myself. Like the fictional mother, I like to be in shape and have good health. Unlike the fictional mother, I have to work at it.

The fictional mother is married to the perfect husband.

Enough said.

The fictional mother faces uncomplicated problems that can usually be solved quickly, often within thirty minutes.

Anything that can be solved in under an hour does not qualify as a real problem, at least not in my life. True, many of my problems have simply disappeared without much effort on my part. Others have taken years to deal with, and still others remain problems, even after years of trying to work them out. My life and the lives of women I know are part order and part chaos. There are certain things that we are good at and have under control. In these areas, we create order and stability. And then there is the rest of life, which is spontaneous and unexpected, sometimes disturbing and sometimes magical, and it will never be different. Life cannot be controlled, no matter who you are. Only in fiction can life be tied up in a neat little bow.

The fictional mother does not experience anxiety, PMS, restlessness, or boredom.
Though these emotional conditions represent only a tiny fraction of a woman's inner life, they are part of what fuels her search for self-knowledge, integration, and wholeness. Interestingly, this search often brings us into conflict with men, many of whom would rather we remain passive and simpleminded. In all too many cases, the inner life of women has been denied or treated as evidence of our emotional instability. The fictional mother has very little inner life. What inner life she has doesn't cause her any great distress or trigger deep self-reflection. In other words, the fictional mother is not a real woman.

As I mentioned earlier, when the country needed women in the factories during World War II, we became working mothers, and no one thought of our services as a betrayal to men or our children. When the men returned from war and it was more "appropriate" from a societal standpoint that they have the factory jobs, we went home to heal the family. Now, at the close of the twentieth century and the birth of the new millennium, we are once more needed as breadwinners, in part because American families need two incomes to support their lifestyle. Women must work so that the family can survive, albeit in a new form. Yet there have been repercussions to our service as income producers, repercussions no one foresaw.

• THE BACKLASH AGAINST THE REAL LIFE OF WOMEN •

No other factor has changed the family more than the working mother. In many cases, both spouses work long hours and are therefore equally absent from the home. But the image of the fictional perfect mother remains very much alive in people's minds, and in an implicit and largely unconscious way, the two-income family has hit the woman's reputation harder than it has the man's. Rather than look upon both working parents with compassion—families are, after all, struggling to survive—our society has subtly condemned women for leaving the home. Many people believe that a woman who maintains her career has essentially abandoned her children.

• THE POWER OF THE IMAGE •

Even though I dismiss the image of the fictional mother as false, I recognize how powerful it is in today's world. We live in a society in which people yearn for images of the mother and for the unconditional love that the archetypal mother offers. In childhood, no relationship is more important to our survival and our mental and emotional health. A mother's love literally shapes and directs the lives of her children. You must be practical in court because it is the arena in which you will either win custodial care of your children or lose it. Therefore, you must adopt the image of that perfect mother and utilize it for your own purposes. You must adopt the dress and the attitude of the ideal mother in order to help you win your case. Anything short of that, in fact, jeopardizes your chances of maintaining the custodial care of your children. In Chapter 8, I show you how you can do exactly that. The reason, very simply, is that if you attempt to present yourself as something other than that in court, you may very well lose your case.

While I express that very practical reality, I am saying that you must not let the image of the perfect mother rob you of all that you are as a mother, and all the appreciation you deserve, especially from yourself. A mother gives so much of herself throughout her children's life, primarily when her children are young. All the love we have given creates a permanent bond with our children, one that, sooner or later, they realize themselves.

• FINDING THE SOURCE OF YOUR GUILT: • THE HIDDEN PERFECT MOTHER WHO JUDGES YOU

As you approach your court date, you must attain the right perspective on your motherhood; you must remember the love you have given and the sacrifices you have made as a mother and then honor yourself for having given so much. You must understand the difference between you and the archetype, just as you must understand the difference between you and the fictional mother. You are the only real mother in your children's lives.

To better understand the source of any guilt you may feel about your role as mother, ask yourself the following questions and answer them as honestly and as thoroughly as you can. Write your answers in a journal or on some paper. As I will describe in greater detail in Chapter 3, you will have to destroy those pages once you have completed them, lest they be discovered and then subpoenaed for your court date. It's important to write out your answers if you can, however. The act of putting down the answers provides you with more insight. You will find yourself being more honest than if you simply thought about your responses. In any case, even if you do not write out your feelings, answer the questions below as thoroughly and honestly as you can. In the process, you will discover and eliminate many of the hidden sources of your feelings of guilt and your self-criticism.

• QUESTIONS AND EXERCISES FOR SELF-DISCOVERY •

1. Find your image of the perfect mother. Describe her in as much detail as you can.
2. What is the source of this woman? Your own mother? Television? Films? Literature?
3. Is she judging a particular action you took or failed to take? What was that act?
4. In addition to judging a particular act or event in your life, is she critical of you in general? If so, what characteristic of yours is she most critical of?
5. Does she come from your own need for mothering?
6. How do you see yourself in relation to this woman? Are you her child? Her sister?
7. How have you sacrificed so that your children would have a better life?
8. How have you tried to give your children love and care in the ways your mother didn't give you?
9. How would you like to give them more now?

• DEALING WITH GUILT •

These questions are arranged in such a way as to help you identify the critical mother image, identify the act or characteristic in you that she is most critical of, see your own need for mothering, start on the process of recognizing how much you have done and how much you have sacrificed for your children, and start to see a better future for yourself and your children. Once you better understand your inner mother, you must set about releasing yourself from the guilt you feel about not meeting her standards in your role as mother. The first step in doing this is to understand the source of the guilt and then to see, as best you can, all that you have given your children as a mother.

• MOTHERS: THE GIVING TREES •

It all begins, of course, in pregnancy. For all its satisfactions and joys, pregnancy still involves a sacrifice of the body, mind, and heart. Women have ancient and archetypal memories deep in our brains that remind us that women throughout human existence have died in pregnancy. We know on some level that this is a dangerous time for us and the child we nurture inside of us. Yet in our own ways, we place our lives second to that of the growing child within.

During pregnancy, through some miracle or unknown alchemy, you grow into the knowledge that your child, growing inside of you, is you—and yet is somehow more than you. He shares your blood, your body, your mind; his entire world is defined by all that you feel and do. Your joy is her joy, your sadness her sadness, your fears her fears. Conversely, you are aware that his or her life is also independent from your own. When your baby is born, you nurse her from your breasts or bottle-feed her in your arms. You are up at night—sometimes all night long—and rise early in the morning to care for her again. You put away your own desires, your own needs, in favor of this child. You are a mother first, an individual woman second—often a distant second. Again and again you forget that you exist in any way that is separate from this child, whom you love more than your own life.

As your child grows, you nurture him as best you can. You try to create order in his life, even when there is little order in your own. You try to understand him even when all that he does baffles and confuses you. You try to be calm and strong even as you are afraid for him. You love him with all your heart, even when he has angered you or made you sad or reflected back at you your own worst characteristics and behavior.

In the midst of all these demands come moments of great joy, happiness, and satisfaction. There are times when your children delight you so much or make you so proud or so happy that you can hardly believe they came from you. Do you even dare to claim, if only in some small way, that you had a hand in shaping such beauty?

Motherhood is filled with contradictions—joys that last forever and conflicts that are never solved. As a mother, you hold these paradoxes in your heart. Somehow all of your memories of happiness and sorrow combine to transform you until the only judgment that you have of your children, the only one that really matters, is love.

It's no wonder that our very planet is referred to as mother earth, because like the earth itself, mothers are asked to bear and endure and carry all things, as we give love. And after we have given all this love, we must perform the hardest sacrifice of all: We must let these children go.

Of course we fail at perfection. We are imperfect women, married to imperfect men, raising imperfect children, tied to imperfect jobs, living imperfect lives. Motherhood is a call to self-sacrifice even as our humanity demands that we remain intact and self-aware. Motherhood demands that we identify so thoroughly with our children that we sacrifice ourselves for their good, while at the same time respect and remember their boundaries and our own. We are called to give all we can, but we ultimately pull back, restore our individuality and their own, so that they can go off as separate human beings. Who can perform such feats without making mistakes? It's no wonder that so many great mothers of history have been granted divine status, are referred to as goddesses. The job of being a mother is beyond the reach of most mere mortals.

Yet we do our best. And we succeed more than we know. The real challenge every mother faces is to honor herself and the great love she has given, even as she compares herself to an unsustainable standard of perfection.

•   •   •

As a daughter, I did not care if my mother sewed the buttons on my dress or made cookies. What I wanted was for her to be truly present and to give me all her attention whenever she was with me, even if it was just for an hour or two a week. My mother was addicted to drugs and alcohol. Much of the time we were together, she was intoxicated, which brought out the worst in her. But even more damaging than her behavior, I believe, was the fact that she never really saw the real me. When I was a teenager, I realized that I was not being seen. How could she be a mother to me if she never actually sees me? I remember thinking. Yet my mother did love me, I believe. That was an essential revelation in my life—that despite all the pain we experienced in our relationship, my mother loved me and wanted me to be happy, even if she couldn't give me happiness.

I have not been an ideal mother, especially when I compare myself to the fictional ideal. I don't cook, I've never made cookies, and I don't sew either. Yet I gave my children many things my mother never gave me. One of them was the gift of my attention. It's true that much of my time was taken up by my job and my harried life. And these rob both men and women of their awareness of their children. But I have tried to be with my children, really be present with them, as much as I could, and in those moments I have communicated both that I see them—each one individually—and, more important, that I love them with all my heart.

Over the years, I have tried as best I could to be present with them and for them, to give them my love when they were sick or emotionally upset or when they were successful. Love comes in many forms—as praise, understanding, solace, a loving touch, a loving voice, physical care, and a consistent belief in their talents, abilities, and inherent goodness. While I have not been a woman free of anxieties or troubles, I have still managed to give my children all that I have to give. I have vicariously suffered their pain and experienced their elation. A mother cannot help but be one with her children. In the end, I gave myself as best I could.

Having the right perspective on your role as mother—that is, being secure in your role and largely free of guilt—is essential for the next step in your effort to gain custody of your children. That next step is documenting your role as mother in the lives of your children.

3 PROVING YOUR FITNESS AS A MOTHER

After I hired an attorney and unsuccessfully attempted to settle with my husband, I mistakenly believed that I could turn over the reins of my case to my lawyer. I quickly learned otherwise. Soon my husband, through his attorney, fired off a volley of charges against me, the sum of which was that I was mentally unfit to raise our children and that I was limiting his visitation rights. He cited my eating disorder, which he knew I had overcome, as evidence of my instability. He also said that I made it difficult for him to see his children, and by doing that, I had violated our divorce agreement.

The dragon had appeared, I thought. The eating disorder was out of the closet. They had their weapon. I felt small and terrified, and something inside me knew that more was to come. How was I going to prove my fitness as a parent? I asked myself. Everything he knows about me, every fault, both real and invented, is going to come out and be exposed in front of a judge. I pictured the judge slamming down his gavel and taking away my children. I felt like the proverbial deer in the headlights—caught in the open and defenseless. All my worst fears were being realized.

It took me a few days before I was able to start to think clearly again. When I did, I realized that I couldn't rely on my attorney to shield me from the attacks that would come from my former husband. I also realized that if my lawyer was going to argue effectively for my worthiness as a mother, I would have to give him the proof that he needed. How can such a thing be proven? I asked myself again. I also worried about how I could actually prove that I was not limiting my former husband's access to his children. Wouldn't our respective claims all boil down to his word against mine? After thinking about it for a while, the answer finally came to me: I would have to document everything I did as a mother and as a responsible woman. I would literally have to make a record of my life, my children's lives, and the visits they had with their father.

The act of documenting my life soon became the basis for my defense. It also became a daily practice that kept me grounded in my central purpose—winning my custody battle. The record I established gave me the proof I needed to combat my husband's charges against me. With such documentation, I had a physical record, undeniable proof that my children were cared for; that they were doing well in school; and that I was a responsible and devoted mother. I also kept a record of all my interactions with my former husband, as well as my children's interactions with him. In this way, I could show that I was not in any way impeding his access to his children.

But documenting my life gave me benefits that I would never have guessed beforehand. Without doing this very practical work, I would never have had anything concrete with which to combat my fear of my former husband's attacks against me. Now I had something that, even if it was never used in court, gave me a sense of security, something very real and tangible that I could use to defend myself. This practice also gave me a sense of power. It was something I could do in the face of my husband's threats. I was fighting back—not with angry words or deeds, but with something real that would stand up in court, if need be. Court was the ultimate arena. Any action that would not stand up in court was meaningless, I realized. A record of my life as a mother could be admitted as evidence that I was a competent parent. That made it powerful and, by extension, gave me power. I did not have to be a victim.

Finally, by creating a record of all that I was doing as a mother, I was able to keep my relationship with my former husband clear and businesslike. Indeed, the record-keeping had a strange effect on my relationship with him. It gave me an objectivity that was also a source of power. Either he showed up to see the children when he said he would or he didn't; either he made child support payments or he didn't. It was all recorded. The issues between us now were reduced to simple yeses and nos; it was all very black and white, all of it written down in my record. Eventually, the record would be presented in court, where it would influence a judge's decision.

Often visitation rights are cited as the cause of the suit when in fact there is some other reason your former husband is trying to secure custody of your children. Sometimes the hidden motive is his lingering resentment toward you, a desire for revenge, or a distorted way of getting you back as his wife. Try as best you can to ferret out the true reason. Keeping the kind of record I describe below will help you identify the hidden motive, or at the very least help you sweep away any claim he might make that you are restricting his access to his children. Discuss the reasons you think your husband is suing for custody with your lawyer. With this knowledge, the two of you may be able to devise a strategy that might lead to a settlement and the avoidance of a court battle.

Documenting my life as a mother, my children's lives, and their relationship with their father was the next step in the process of winning custodial care of my children. I urge that you make it yours. As you will see, this will help you regain your power and achieve your objective.

• START IMMEDIATELY AFTER YOUR DIVORCE •

Keep the kind of record I describe below from the time you are divorced. I had been divorced for more than two years when my husband decided to sue for custody of our children. His actions came as a complete surprise to me and I was totally unprepared for them. The ostensible reason for his suit was a letter I wrote to him asking that we follow some ground rules for visitation. One of my requests was that he give me adequate notice before coming to the house to pick up the children. At that point, he had unlimited access to our kids and he was falling into the habit of calling unexpectedly, often at the last minute, to say that he wanted to come over and pick up the children. That wasn't working for any of us; the children were often out of the house when he called and sometimes his calls conflicted with my own plans. I also wanted to set up a predictable visitation schedule—say, every other weekend, for example, or something that we both could count on. There was no schedule at the time; visitation was based more on his schedule than anyone else's.

I explicitly encouraged him to keep seeing the children. I was only seeking an orderly and predictable schedule for visitation.

As understandable as these requests might seem, they infuriated him and served as the basis for his accusation that I was limiting his access to the children. I was making it difficult and sometimes even impossible for him to see his children, he said. His only recourse was to sue me for custody. Of course, I had not been keeping any record of his visits. Consequently, I could not prove that he was seeing his children; nor could I prove that his demands were unpredictable and unfair.

Three lessons come out of my experience. The first is this: Once you are divorced, be extremely careful of what you write to your former husband, especially when it concerns his visiting the children and anything to do with your personal life. Second, save copies of all correspondence between the two of you once you are divorced. Third, start to keep the kind of record I describe as soon as you are divorced. This is a simple way of protecting yourself against the day when you are served court papers that you never expected to see.

• DETERMINING YOUR FITNESS AS A PARENT •

The principle that guides a judge's decision over who will gain custody of the children is captured in the phrase "the best interests of the child." There are two general areas that the judge will examine to determine how the best interests of your children are served. The first is whether you or your former husband is the more fit parent. The second is which of you is more likely to comply with the court's visitation order. This means that if you are deemed more likely to allow your former spouse to see his children in the way the court has mandated, then you will have met this criterion and therefore be the one more likely to be granted custodial rights.

In one way or another, most of the key issues fall under these two general categories. The court uses the following specific criteria to determine your fitness as a parent, as well as that of your former husband.

- Whether or not you or your former husband has been convicted of a felony. In most states, a felony conviction automatically rules a parent out as the primary custodial caretaker.
- Evidence that you or your former husband is neglecting or abusing your children. If proven, such abuse requires a judge to remove the children from your or your former husband's custody.
- Evidence that you have abused your former husband or he has abused you. Spousal abuse will bring about the loss of custody.
- The length of time the children have resided with you or your husband. Continuity of the existing conditions—and by extension, a child's experience of family—is important to the court.
- Your children's psychological health. Very likely, they will be tested extensively by court-appointed psychologists who will determine whether or not they are thriving under your care, if you are currently the custodial parent. (See Chapter 7 for more on testing of your children.)

- Your children's performance at school.
- Your children's behavior in the community. If the child has been in trouble with the law or arrested, the judge may view this behavior as a direct result of poor parenting and therefore turn over the custodial privileges to the nonresidential parent.
- Your financial circumstances, especially as they relate to your capacity to provide your children with food, clothing, shelter, medical care, and other material needs.
- Your and your former husband's moral character. This includes the people and influences you and your former husband bring into the children's lives as a consequence of your respective lifestyles, including your respective sex lives. Your sex life will be closely scrutinized by the court, by court-appointed psychologists, and by the court's family services. Sexual relationships can hurt your case, particularly premarital sex that takes place in your home. You may think that you can keep some areas of your life private and perhaps even secret. I urge you to act as if everything you do will become public and therefore known to the court, because chances are it will.
- The mental and physical health of the parents. You and your former husband will be interviewed extensively by the family court services and court-appointed psychologists. These reports will have a bearing on the judge's ultimate decision. (More on the family court services and court-appointed psychologists in Chapter 7.)
- Evidence that either of you knowingly provided false information to the court regarding spousal or child abuse. If you or your husband accuses the other of any form of abuse, that person had better be able to prove it. If either of you makes such an accusation and cannot prove it, he or she will very likely lose the custody suit.
- Compliance with the visitation rights of the nonresidential parent. The judge will determine which of you is more likely to allow visitation and continuing contact with the nonresidential

parent. This is a strong factor in the judge's decision and will weigh very heavily in the compliant parent's favor. As mentioned above, if you are preventing your former husband from seeing his children or are restricting his visitation rights in any way, you could also lose custody of your children. Do not under any circumstances make the claim that you are restricting your husband's access because he is abusive to his children or to you, unless you have irrefutable proof of such behavior. That proof must become part of your record.

- The parent the children wish to live with. The judge will take into account which parent the children say they want to live with. This is especially true for children who are deemed sufficiently aware and intelligent and who have a strong preference for one or the other parent. The children's choice of parent will be given significant weight among all the other factors. On the other hand, do not under any circumstances attempt to influence your children by speaking ill of their father. Even if you do this surreptitiously, it will very likely be discovered by the court-appointed psychologists and family services personnel and will ultimately go against you in court.
- The love, affection, and emotional ties the children have to one or both of the parents. Such information is usually elicited during psychological testing.

Finally, the judge has enormous discretion to consider anything he or she deems relevant to the issue of custody and will include all evidence gleaned from family court services and psychological interviews.

Your job is to prove you are the more worthy parent by documenting your fitness in these areas. Here's how you can do that.

• DOCUMENTING YOUR LIFE AS A SINGLE PARENT •

The act of documenting your life as a parent is not as difficult as you might think. What it requires more than anything else is organization and the ability to keep track of certain key events and details. After a while it becomes a habit, a good one. Essentially, you are going to document several areas of your children's lives, their relationship with their father, and your schedule.

Here are the pieces of equipment and supplies you will need.

A CAMERA THAT PROVIDES A DATE ON PHOTOGRAPHS TAKEN

The first thing I would urge you to do is buy a camera that dates the photographs. Ideally, you would use this camera to take a photograph of your husband with his children whenever he visits. That's not always possible. Instead, make every effort to take photographs at key events, such as holidays and birthdays. The photograph produced will have a date on it, which will serve as proof that your husband is seeing his children, especially at important points in their lives, such as birthdays.

In my own case, my husband attempted to prove that he had not seen his children during the Christmas holidays because I was preventing him from visiting. My attorneys produced photographs of my husband with his children at Christmas. The date appeared directly on the photograph.

Finally, the camera should be used in the event that one or more of your children returns from a visit with their father bruised or beaten. Such abuse should be documented and then brought to the attention of your attorney immediately.

THE CHILDREN'S CALENDAR AND JOURNAL

You will need a calendar that offers room to make notes on each date and a bound notebook, such as a composition book. I refer to this calendar as the children's calendar. It should not be used for any of your personal or professional events or scheduling. Rather, it should be used only to keep track of your husband's telephone calls, visits to his children, and the children's events, such as school field trips, choir concerts, music lessons, extracurricular activities, and/or religious events.

The calendar can be kept openly, say, on your kitchen wall, but the journal should be kept private if at all possible. You do not want to give your children the impression that you are spying on them or that you are using them to defeat their father in court. Of the two forms of record-keeping, the calendar is much more important than the journal. The journal is especially useful if your children are regularly upset by their father or verbally or physically abused by him. The journal can be used to document what the children reported about these instances and then turned over to your lawyer for further action.

For mothers whose former spouses are not abusive, however, the most important information to be recorded is your former husband's contacts with his children. On the calendar, note the date and the duration of your former husband's visit to his children, or theirs to him. Note any upcoming visits with their father and whether they actually occurred.

Keep track of the telephone calls in the same way. Indicate the date of the call, the time it occurred, and how long it lasted. In your notebook, document any reaction your children exhibit or express to you about the call. If you have more than one child, note whether your former husband talked to all his children and how they reacted to the call. Be sure to note *all* their reactions, both the negative and the positive ones. If it was a good call, say so in your book. If they argued, write it down. If your child shares the details of that argument, write those down as well. Don't worry if you don't record a reaction to every call or you miss some calls. It doesn't matter. Keep the record as best you can. Some parents like to call on a particular night, such as Tuesdays or

Thursdays. If such a pattern is established, it's easier for you to keep track of the calls. In any case, a pattern of emotions eventually establishes itself. If your former husband is calling regularly and the children feel good about his calls and their relationship with him, this will be evident, just as its opposite will be. Allow the facts to emerge and record them honestly.

Very important: Do not pry into your children's feelings. Do not use them to gain information about their father. Usually the children feel their loyalties so divided between the two of you that they can't bring themselves to let one of you know what the other might have said. That's fine. Very often, it's also healthy. Don't push them. Let them know that you are there if they need to talk, that you want to help them with their feelings if something bothers them, but that you respect their privacy. They are more likely to talk to you if you are supportive and open to them, but respectful of their love for their father. Teenagers especially need to know you are granting them their freedom and respecting their boundaries. (More on your relationship with your children during this difficult time in Chapter 5.)

What matters most in this record is that it shows that you are allowing him all the access he wants. He visits and telephones the children often. They visit and call him. No one is preventing him from having a close relationship with his children. Your children's calendar and journal are proof that he has free and frequent access to his children. Moreover, if he doesn't visit or call his children, it is not because you are limiting his visitation or calls in any way.

THE CHILDREN'S FILES

Buy a cardboard file box, if you haven't already got a filing cabinet, and a box of file folders to store and organize your paperwork. Create a separate file folder for each of the following categories of information.

- Letters and e-mails you write to your former husband. Very likely, you will occasionally have to write to your former husband about scheduling children's visits or some concern you may have regarding the children. Perhaps one of the children is having trouble in school; or is doing very well in school and is receiving an award; or has an important school event coming up that your former husband should know about and perhaps attend. Or perhaps you have an important business meeting coming up that conflicts with his visitation or with your plans to deliver the children on a particular date. If you are not comfortable calling your former husband—and chances are you won't be, especially if he is suing you for custody—then you'll probably want to write him a letter.

  First, be sure that you keep your letters objective, business-like, and strictly factual. Do not show any emotions, especially anger or feelings of revenge. Above all, do not write anything that might be construed as an effort to limit his visitation. On the contrary, you should appear in these letters as willing to do whatever it takes to foster your children's relationship with their father.

  If you have any doubts about the content of any letter you write to your husband, show it to your lawyer before sending it. The letters that you write will turn up in court. You will need a copy of everything you write.

- Letters and e-mails he writes to you. As with your letters to your former husband, be sure to share all his correspondence with your attorney.

- All correspondence to and from your attorney.

- All correspondence to and from your former husband's attorney. It's very unlikely you will receive a letter directly from your former husband's attorney that your own lawyer will not receive, but check with your lawyer to be sure that he received a copy of the latest correspondence from your husband's attorney. If he hasn't, make a copy and send it to him. He should then contact your former spouse's attorney and ask that copies of all correspondence be sent to him.

- Court documents and reports, including reports from the family court services and psychologists (those who interview you, your husband, and your children).

- School report cards for each child. Each child should have his or her own separate folder to hold copies of all his or her report cards over the period of your custody suit. My custody suit ran over a two-year period, so there were numerous report cards for each of my three children. Most report cards must be signed and sent back to school; make copies of them before they go back and file the copies away.

  Include copies of report cards from the time before your custody suit began. This is especially important if your husband sues for custody after you have been divorced for some time and the children are living with you. If the report cards show grade-level work or above, they demonstrate that your children were excelling academically while under your care. That's the purpose of this file: to show that you are making sure that your children are thriving academically, even while you are embroiled in a difficult custody battle. Such records exhibit your care and commitment to their development and future.

- A separate file folder for each child's schoolwork. You can break down these folders into specific subject areas, such as math, science, social studies, English, secondary languages (such as French, Spanish, or Latin, if the children are studying any), and art. These folders need not include every homework assignment, but should contain representative samples from each course. Be sure to include any term papers, reports, or projects on which your child did especially well.

- Records of absence, tardiness, and interactions with teachers. Keep a record of all teacher conferences you attend and anything your children's teachers report about the children's progress in school. These conferences are good ways to keep abreast of how your child is doing in school, where he or she is excelling, and where he or she may need extra help. If the situation allows, tell the teacher that your child may be under more stress of late because of your custody battle. This may be especially important if you have young children in grammar school. Keep all notes that teachers send home and record any follow-up you engaged in.

Pay close attention to your children's progress in school and note if they need special tutoring or remedial classes. Keep records of any additional programs or tutoring that you arrange for your children

Record any extended periods of absence from school, such as from sickness, and any tardiness and the reasons for such lateness. School attendance and tardiness often come up in court as evidence that your children are not excelling in school or that you are neglecting your duties in some way. Be sure that if they do miss school or are tardy, you have an explanation for such events and that they are short-lived.

- Records of field trips. This serves as proof that you are involved in your children's lives, both at home and at school. It reminds the judge that you are your own version of the perfect mother.
- Records of extracurricular activities in which your children are involved. Soccer, basketball, tennis, football, choir, music lessons—anything and everything your kids are involved in outside of school must be noted. It shows that they have a full and active life under your care.
- Awards from school and other activities that your children receive. These provide more evidence that they are excelling at life.
- Medical and dental records. All your trips to the doctor and dentist must be recorded and filed away. With each note you make for your child's visit to a doctor or dentist, be sure to include the reason for the visit. Note any special treatments your child needs, such as from a particular hospital or specialist. Include receipts for all out-of-pocket payments made by you.

Very important: include all wellness checkups and visits to the dentists. This demonstrates your conscientiousness when it comes to maintaining your children's health.

- Vacation photographs and memorabilia. Document your family vacations or weekend trips with photographs and dates (the photographs should have dates on them, as described above).
- An outline of at least one month's worth of living expenses for your children and you, complete with receipts that document all essential purchases. This file should demonstrate typical monthly expenses. It should include rent/mortgage, food, clothing, heat and utilities, medical and dental bills, children's social functions, gasoline, credit cards, unexpected costs (which arise almost monthly, as every mother knows), and your own clothing (a word of advice: keep this figure low, since a large amount causes suspicion that you are using child support to enhance your wardrobe).

This record forms the foundation for your claims for child support. You compile it to show how expensive life is today for a single mother and her children, and how essential child support really is.

- Receipts for a second phone line from a hall or child's room where the children can call their father in privacy. This is evidence that you are promoting your children's relationship with their father and giving the children and their father privacy to boot. You are not interfering, the phone line says. You want them to have a close relationship, one free of any interference by you.
- Copies of phone bills showing their calls to him. One of the best documents for proving that he is regularly in touch with his children, or is not in touch by his own choice.
- Copies of photographs you take of your husband's visits with his children.
- Records of the children's social life and special costs. Receipts, ticket stubs, and costs for specific social functions, such presents

you had to purchase for birthday parties; costumes; valentines; gifts to teachers; gifts for bar mitzvahs; confirmation gifts; Christmas gifts to friends. Also included in this file should be receipts for special tools or supplies needed by the children, such as a computer, printer, computer paper, and related supplies.

Children have many different needs that are unique to them. My children play instruments, which are costly. No doubt your children have special needs and talents that cost you money. Note all of these costs in this file and in your typical monthly expenses file as well.

You will also need a large three-ring binder with dividers and pouches. This you will use to bring some of your information to court. Another essential item is a personal organizer or personal calendar to demonstrate how you are using your time, including how you spend your free time.

• YOUR LIFE: AN OPEN BOOK AND ON THE RECORD •

Once divorced, a single mother must be very careful about her relationships, especially those with men. She must avoid exposing her children to any hint of impropriety, however vague or innocent it might be. Any indiscretion can be used against her by her former husband, who will try to convince the court that she is raising their children in a morally bankrupt environment.

On one of the family court services documents, my former husband referred to me as a bimbo and alluded to my sex life. His allegations were not based on any facts—believe me, he would have used them had he had them—but on his suspicions. After my divorce, I did occasionally go out on a date. I did not bring a man to my home. Yet because my husband called one night and was told by my children that I was out on a date, I suddenly became a promiscuous single mother, a bimbo. This pejorative reference reflected badly on him, of course, but it served a purpose: It alerted the court family service personnel and court-appointed psychologists to examine my sex life carefully. It raised a red flag that I might be exposing my children to immoral situations.

Keep in mind that one of the primary factors that the court will use to determine your worthiness as a parent is your moral character, at least as it is judged by the court. Moral character is a very broad term that can include many aspects of your life, but one of the big ones, as you well know, is your sex life. Be extremely circumspect about your dating and your relationships with men—or with women, for that matter.

There is nothing inherently wrong with your going out and even dating. Very often, it's more a matter of perception than substance. Remember, you are being compared against the court's image of the perfect mother. The perfect mother doesn't bring men home, especially to sleep in her bed; she doesn't allow her children to see a man she isn't married to at the breakfast table; and she doesn't expose them to any knowledge of her sex life. If you do any of these things and your former husband finds out about it—and such information is virtually impossible to keep from him, especially if your children don't approve of your behavior—then it will be used against you in court.

An affair does not automatically disqualify you from retaining custodial care of your children, but it doesn't support your case, either. What matters most, attorneys point out, is your discretion. If you keep the affair private and out of the view of your children, you are on much safer ground. But if you flaunt your affair or expose your children to behavior that the court might deem harmful or embarrassing to your children, you may very well lose your case. Your former husband and his attorney will argue that your behavior is not in the best interests of your children, and depending on the circumstances, the judge could very well agree with them.

Now the truth may be that you have fallen in love with your soul mate or that you need company and a confidant during a very difficult time. In any case, you may feel strongly that no one has a right to control your life—which is true—but make no mistake, a child custody hearing is *not* a fair process. You must understand, as I tried to point out earlier, the woman is held to a higher standard than the man in a custody suit. The most important objective in this process is that you win custody of your children. Your social life can easily cause you to make mistakes, sometimes fatal ones, which the court will not forgive. As long as you can account for your time and demonstrate that your children are not being neglected in the least, you will be safe from excessive judgment.

This is especially the case if you are a lesbian or have had a homosexual relationship. In many states, a woman's sexual preference is relevant only insofar as it affects the general well-being of her children. If she is discreet and does not expose her children to situations that might prove harmful or embarrassing to them, her sexual orientation and lifestyle are not considered important. Other states, however, view things very differently. They consider a person's sexual preference a fundamental part of character and morality and regard homosexuality as a direct and often detrimental influence on a child's life. As I mentioned earlier, judges have a wide latitude; they can allow their own biases to influence their decision as well.

My advice to all women involved in a custody suit—no matter what your sexual orientation may be—is keep all love affairs secret, especially from your children and your former husband. If you are a lesbian, do not flaunt it, especially during the period of the trial. Keep your relationships private and out of sight of the children and your former husband. Even if you live in a liberal state, your sexual orientation may cause a judge to look more sympathetically on your husband and his former life with you. Under no circumstances should you have a live-in partner, at least until after your case has been resolved. The same advice goes for heterosexual women. Do not live with a man out of wedlock while you are engaged in this battle. Even more important, do not flaunt your sexuality.

If your former husband has any suspicions about your sex life, no matter what your orientation may be, he will likely use it against you in court. It's very important, therefore, for you to keep your own personal organizer book or calendar that demonstrates that you are home virtually every evening, and that even on nights you may go out with friends or on a date, you come home that evening after your social event has concluded. Make a little note in your calendar about who is babysitting that night. It doesn't hurt to keep track of the hours you were out, either. There should always be a reference to the fact that the children are well supervised and cared for in your absence.

As I demonstrate in Chapters 7 and 8, much depends on how you present yourself to the family court services, the court-appointed psychologists, and the judge. The clothes you wear, the way you conduct yourself during these interviews, and how you present yourself in court will all color the way people see the actual facts of your life. Behavior that is innocent must be reinforced by the way you hold yourself during these interviews and court sessions.

• THE PROOF IS IN THE RECORD •

This record is proof of your dedication as a mother. It shows how you use your energy, time, and money. It documents and proves your love. But it is also an important way of diffusing fear, which is the next subject that we must address on our journey to a victory in court.

4 HOW TO DIFFUSE THE FEAR OF LOSING YOUR CHILDREN AND GET THE SUPPORT YOU NEED

The first thing you have to do with fear is acknowledge that it's there. The second is to know its source. Unless you are in some kind of imminent physical danger—someone is holding a knife to your throat or a car is rushing at you—then the source of your fear is some picture of the future in your mind. The truth is, there are any number of possible futures you could experience. Some of them are downright terrifying, it's true, but some are truly wonderful. It's up to you to help create the latter. You can start to do that by realizing that your fears are based on a picture of the future you are conjuring up and believing in. If you believe in those pictures strong enough, they will cripple you. They will prevent you from doing all you can to create your victory. Eventually you may even contribute to making your fears a reality.

The first thing you must realize about the picture-making machine in your head is this: The more passive you are, the more negative pictures it generates. This is a vicious cycle. The more you run away from your problems, the more they overwhelm you. On the other hand, you can't always be engaged in the fight. It will wear you out and the stress will become overwhelming. You've got to take a yin-yang approach to the problem. By this I mean you have to engage the problem aggressively—you must be yang some of the time—and then you have to back off, retreat and escape to a comfortable distance so that you can support and replenish yourself. In other words, be yin.

In Chapter 3 I described an aggressive, power-enhancing array of activities. The more you do them, the more under control your case will feel. In time, you will feel that you not only deserve to win but have the proof necessary to prevail. The activities I describe in the chapters on dealing with your former husband, the family court services, and the court itself are also power-enhancing. In this chapter, I want to show you that you can strengthen your will and reduce fear by taking good care of yourself. These activities will also strengthen your case, some of them directly, others indirectly.

My technique to reduce fear and powerlessness is based on six steps. They are as follows:

1. Create order in your life.
2. Strengthen your body.
3. Strengthen your mind.
4. Use social support.
5. Strengthen your spirit.
6. Enjoy guilty pleasures—without the guilt.

These six steps tend to be cumulative in their effects. By this I mean that they are far more powerful when used together than when you use only one or two of them.

Let's look at each step individually.

• 1. CREATE ORDER IN YOUR LIFE •

Few things are more destabilizing and disempowering than chaos. Fear promotes chaos and loss of control. Once chaos sets in, it triggers more fear and more chaos, and thus a vicious cycle sets in. On the other hand, gaining a sense of control gives you a feeling that life is in balance and that your problems, whatever they may be, are manageable.

Feeling in control in one or two areas of your life makes you feel more in control of your life overall. Most of us feel safer and more secure when our homes are orderly and clean, when our schedules are constant and under our control, and when we perceive that our children are safe.

During my custody suit, my children were ages fourteen, twelve, and ten, which meant that they had school and homework five days a week for ten months per year. Most days they would come to my office after school. From there we would all go out for a snack before we went home. Once at home, the children would go out with friends or do their homework. At night, I would be home or seeing clients at my office. If I was working, the children had to be home unless we had already agreed on other plans. I insisted on curfews during the week and on weekends. During the summer, I often left for work before they got up, but I could get free during the day—sometimes for whole days—to take them to the beach. We had a summer curfew that they usually complied with as well.

It's very important that your children agree to certain ground rules. Obviously, you can overdo it and cause your children to rebel, but in most cases children will comply with certain fundamental rules, especially if you stress that you need these structures to help you maintain order and safety in all of your lives.

Keep in mind that your children need organization in order to succeed in school. They need time to do their homework and to study for tests. Their schoolwork and grades will be looked at as indications of your competency as a mother. If they are doing well in school, you will be seen as promoting good values and a stable home. But if they are doing poorly in school, you may be seen as incapable of creating order and a lifestyle that is in your children's long-term best interests. Therefore, no matter how orderly or disorderly you may be with your life, make sure that your children have enough order in theirs to keep their grades up.

Everyone has her own sense of what she needs to maintain order in her life. Ask yourself which areas of your life you can get better under your control to enhance your sense of security. Don't try to control the areas you cannot. In other words, don't ask the impossible of yourself. On the contrary, choose the smaller parts of your day that you can control and then use them to create a sense of stability in your life.

• 2. STRENGTHEN YOUR BODY •

During this period of great stress you must do all you can to support yourself, in particular to support your health. The words "do all you can" are not meant to be interpreted as "do more than you can." You don't need another set of headaches or anyone telling you to be better than you are. On the contrary, if anything, you need someone to tell you how wonderful and courageous you are. All I want is to help you find effective ways of diminishing your fear. The tools I suggest worked for me. I believe they will work for you.

Essentially, there are three approaches to your body that will help you control fear and make you feel stronger. These are exercise, diet, and the use of helper-healers. By using all three to whatever extent you can, you can transform your physical appearance as well as your inner and outer lives.

EXERCISE: A LITTLE CAN CHANGE YOUR LIFE

Fear and stress cause your muscles to contract, creating tension in your shoulders, for example, or in your lower back, stomach, or pelvis. When stress becomes chronic, muscles go into spasm and lose their elasticity. Once muscles remain contracted, they prevent blood from flowing optimally through your veins. Cells become deprived of blood and oxygen, and diseases start to manifest.

You experience that muscle contraction as physical tension. Many of us deal with that tension by eating foods that make us feel weak and fat. What most of us don't realize is that the more tension the body holds, the more fear we experience. Conversely, the stronger and more flexible your body is, the less fear you experience. Instead, you feel more powerful, disciplined, and capable of winning your custody suit.

You can significantly improve your health and fitness—in fact, you can change your life—simply by walking a minimum of thirty minutes a day at a fairly brisk pace. I tend to be a nervous, active person, so I had to do more to burn off all the fear and stress I was feeling. In addition to walking, I joined a gym and went at least three times a week to walk on the Stairmaster or the treadmill and then lift weights.

I highly recommend a treadmill and weight lifting. I lift only small weights—I'm not interested in becoming a body builder— but as a result of this activity I feel much more powerful. In fact, a thirty-minute walk on the treadmill and then fifteen minutes of weight lifting will make you feel much more powerful—and power is the point, ladies! You're not going to experience your power sitting on the couch. In fact, inactivity in the face of fear is disastrous; it will only make you feel weaker and more like a victim. Lifting weights significantly improves your muscle tone, tightens your body, strengthens your bones, and makes you feel stronger; and they give you a sense that you are more grounded and are taking up more space on the earth.

As you may know, exercise also changes your brain chemistry and increases production of endorphins, which are naturally occurring chemicals in your brain that make you feel a greater sense of well-being and optimism. Numerous studies have shown that when people with chronic depression exercise, a significant number experience a dramatic elevation of mood and the elimination of depression.

You don't have to limit yourself to weights and walking. Lots of women get the same results I have described by taking martial arts, yoga, aerobics, kickboxing, or tennis, or by joining a walking club. Most Ys have their own fitness clubs that you can join for a nominal fee; often that fee will be reduced for single mothers who want to work out. Health and fitness clubs are often far less expensive than you might think. But you can walk and create your own weights by placing sand or water in empty one-gallon water bottles, which typically have handles. A lack of money shouldn't prevent you from getting all the exercise you need.

DIET: FEAR'S FUEL OR ITS ANTIDOTE

I struggled for sixteen years with an eating disorder and have spent the last eleven years trying to get my diet right. I'm still not entirely comfortable with food because of my eating patterns. In other words, I know better than most how difficult food is, how much we use it to love ourselves, and how essential it is for us to be gentle with ourselves on the subject of diet. Not only am I in no position to preach to you about what you should and should not eat, but I have no interest in doing that, in part because I know how much guilt most of us feel around food. I will not add to your guilt, nor to my own.

On the other hand, I have a lot of experience trying to overcome problems with food. I would like to share some of that experience with you in the hopes that it may help you reduce your tension and fear while it promotes your sense of well-being.

- First, consider reducing or eliminating stimulants, especially coffee and cola drinks. I urge every woman in a custody battle to give up coffee and, instead, drink black tea or herbal tea. A cup of coffee, as you may know, contains anywhere from 100 to 150 milligrams of caffeine. Many people report that two cups of coffee increases their anxiety and physical tension. A cup of tea contains about 45 milligrams of caffeine. Most herbal teas are noncaffeinated. Tea also contains an abundance of anti-oxidants and bioflavonoids that boost your immune system and help you prevent disease.

- Be moderate in your consumption of alcohol. It contributes to or creates depression in many people. It also makes many of us feel physically and mentally weaker.
- Find your own carbohydrate and protein balance. We live at a time when nutritionists and dietary experts tout an enormous variety of dietary regimens. Some say that you should eat a diet high in carbohydrates; others say that you should concentrate on eating lots of protein. There's only one way to find the right answer: You must discover what's right for you.

I do recommend that you try to eat more whole, unprocessed carbohydrate foods, such as brown rice, fresh vegetables, beans, and fruit. These foods provide long-lasting energy, as opposed to the rapidly absorbed sugars in processed foods, such as rolls, bread, pastries, and white sugar, which give you an initial burst of energy but are quickly burned off or stored, possibly resulting in low blood sugar. Low blood sugar is associated with fatigue, moodiness, nervous tension, increased stress and fear, and a sense of powerlessness.

No matter what else you eat, try to eat whole grains, fresh vegetables, and fruit as often as you can. If you eat sugar or chocolate or pastries, try to include a whole-grain dish—such as brown rice, barley, millet, oats, or corn—and some fresh vegetables, beans, or fruit that day as well. By doing this, you will not experience the extreme swings in energy and mood that you would if you eat only processed foods.

- Substitute chicken and fish for all forms of red meat as your sources of animal protein. Chicken and fish are lower in fat, especially saturated fats, than most red meats, which have been linked to heart disease and numerous forms of cancer.

• Include tofu, tempeh, and other such sources of protein in your diet. These foods contain plant estrogens, or phytoestrogens, which are mild and protective forms of estrogen that help prevent breast and uterine cancers, osteoporosis, and other serious disorders.

• Take a multivitamin and mineral supplement daily. Vitamins C and E are important antioxidants, which slow the aging process, boost immunity, and protect against disease. Calcium promotes strong bones; magnesium is essential for the body to absorb and utilize calcium; and zinc promotes a strong immune system. Check to be sure your supplement offers these nutrients in dosages close to the recommended daily values. In other words, avoid megadoses of anything.

Books on diet can be helpful because they are so informative, but nothing substitutes for knowing your own body and its dietary needs. Experiment with your food and listen carefully to your body. That's the shortest route to health and far less fear.

FIND A HELPER WITH HEALING HANDS

Someone once said that our "issues are in the tissues," and that, I believe, is a fundamental truth about living in a human body. Somehow, the fears we experience, the behavioral patterns we establish, and the limits we believe in are all woven into our bodies—indeed, into our very tissues. We brace ourselves for trouble by tensing our shoulders or tightening the muscles in the small of our back or pelvis. These become habitual responses until the muscles in these places lose their range of motion; they become habitually tense. If you allow someone with a healing touch to break up and release that tension, you will find that you feel more relaxed and more flexible. But more important, you will feel less afraid. As your fear diminishes, you will feel freer, safer, more stable, and more creative. Indeed, you will feel better about yourself and the world around you.

Because we spend so much time thinking, the experience of being present in and conscious of our bodies is becoming rare. Massage brings us back to ourselves, back to our most immediate reality—the body itself. And it does so in the most tender and loving way. Massage slows down time. It brings us back to the here and now. It puts us in touch with our most basic and essential needs, especially for physical comfort, gentle touch, and compassion. By getting a massage, you are giving yourself that comfort and compassion, both of which will dramatically reduce your fears. Few things are more relaxing than a good massage. Massage therapists of all types are often listed in your telephone book, on bulletin boards at natural foods stores, at fitness clubs, and in local newspapers and magazines.

Other therapeutic forms of healing that can help reduce fear are acupuncture, Chinese herbal medicine, Western herbal medicine, and homeopathy. I urge you to pick up books on these subjects at your local library or bookstore and investigate them if you feel so inclined.

SMALL GIFTS YOU GIVE YOURSELF

Sometimes the small gifts we give ourselves make a big difference in how we see the world. They are little expressions of self-love that elevate our mood and reduce our fears.

You can give yourself—specifically, give your body—little gifts that will change the quality of your life. No matter how bad things were, I still got my hair and nails done; I got a regular facial; and I took lots of aromatherapy and mineral baths. Aromatherapy baths, or the use of essential oils, provide deep relaxation and the elimination of tension.

Every healthy act of comfort and support that you give yourself takes you out of fear and into a state of self-love. During a time when you are being attacked by your former husband, his lawyers, and even court-related officials, few things are more important than that.

• 3. STRENGTHEN YOUR MIND •

One of the most powerful influences on my life during my custody suit were books. Very few things have the same power to reduce fear and support your spirit as books. Read whatever appeals to you—fiction, adventure, romance, or nonfiction. Personally, I love biography and recommend it, especially when you feel oppressed and alone. Reading about the lives of others who have gone through great difficulties and have emerged wiser, stronger, and more whole is a great inspiration. You begin to recognize that pain and strife are part of the human condition and that you are not alone.

If anything qualifies as a dark night of the soul, a custody suit certainly does. This time of hardship can either break our spirits or make us stronger. Reading about the ways in which strong women and men handled periods of great adversity, times when their very souls were about to break, provides perspective on our own torment. It reminds us that the human spirit is extremely resilient. It can bear great stress—not by denying our pain, but by acknowledging it and holding it in a loving and supportive way.

Reading is also a great escape. It's a wonderful way to enter another person's life and world and to leave your own behind, at least for a time. Read whatever you are drawn to, whatever takes you into another world, relieves you of stress, gives you perspective on your own life, and frees you, at least for short periods every day, from your own struggles.

CRY WHENEVER THE SPIRIT MOVES YOU

Do not be afraid to cry—often and a lot. Most women have no trouble releasing their tears, but too many of us think that crying reflects our weakness rather than our strength. We have the courage and the capacity to feel deeply and to honor our feelings. When we sink into our emotions, we are experiencing life in all its diversity, its joys and conflicts. Naturally we cry in the face of life's pain and sadness. But those tears are also our way of releasing that pain and fear. Crying is cleansing, renewing, and restorative. It connects us with our deepest, purest center, the place from which all true healing flows.

• 4. USE SOCIAL SUPPORT •

You might think that the first thing I'd recommend to help you deal with your fears is therapy, but therapy is really dangerous for you right now. As I discuss at length in Chapter 7, your therapist may be forced to testify against you at your custody hearing. You may think that your conversations with your counselor are confidential, but that's not necessarily so. You may be "encouraged"— meaning pressured—by the court into signing a document that releases your therapist from all confidentiality and thereby allows him or her to testify against you. That happened to me.

Therefore, I urge you to be circumspect with therapists. If you really feel you must talk to someone, see that person only as a source of immediate support and limit your discussions to what is taking place right now. Do not get too deeply into your past and do not allow yourself to be analyzed to such an extent that a diagnosis is made of your condition.

The court will require you to fill out a complete financial statement that will document where your money goes each month. If you see a therapist, I urge you to pay for the counseling in cash, and if it's at all possible, do not report to anyone that you are getting professional help. I also urge you to see a woman therapist, one who understands your situation and can be trusted to keep the therapy within the confines that you define.

The best therapy that you can obtain, at least at this time, is from clergy members. Most priests or ministers will counsel you for free. So too will many rabbis. Very often, the support and advice from clergy are comforting and sound. For many, such counseling is all you really need to help get you through this period of your life.

Once your custody suit is completed, of course, you are free to engage in much deeper psychological work. At that point, you can talk at length about your life without fear of having your therapist turn against you in court. Therapy can help heal your wounds and enable you to move on in your life.

SUPPORT GROUPS

I have some of the same concerns about support groups as I do regarding therapists. However, these concerns do not extend to the twelve-step programs, such as Alcoholics Anonymous or Adult Children of Alcoholics, which are designed to get people to listen to one another, rather than to create dialogues. I encourage you to go to a twelve-step program, and if nothing else, just sit and listen. Very often it's enough to know that there are many people struggling with life, as you are, and that you will come through this difficult time. You may also share what you are going through at these meetings. People who attend these groups tend to be nonjudgmental, supportive, and nonintrusive. Not only will you not be judged, but you won't be diagnosed by a professional therapist who might be called into court. The twelve-step programs, therefore, are safe and highly recommended, should you need that kind of support.

FRIENDS AND FAMILY MEMBERS

First, choose your friends wisely. You don't need to be gossiped about. In fact, gossip at this time can be dangerous, especially if the information gets back to your former husband and he summons your so-called friends into court to testify on his behalf. On the other hand, old and trusted friends are truly a gift. Confide in them, by all means, but try hard not to become a burden to anyone. Don't let your relationships become one-way streets. If you are doing some or all of the things I have encouraged you to do in this chapter, you will be strong enough to listen to your friends' problems, and in turn they can listen to yours.

Just as you must choose your friends wisely, so too must you choose whom to speak to within your family. Those who have a trusted relative, such as an aunt, uncle, brother or sister, mother or father are truly blessed. This is not the case for many people, however. Keep in mind that your need to be listened to and supported is enormous right now. If you have a long-standing issue with a parent or some other relative, I urge you *not* to confide in that person. A family member who harbors a grudge may use the period during which you are vulnerable and open as an opportunity to express his or her own criticisms of you. This could open the door to healing between the two of you, or it may simply be a chance for your relative to hurt you.

Seek out those whose intentions are clearly supportive, people you can trust and to whom you can open your soul. Ask permission to share your concerns and also ask if you can speak to this person on a regular basis. Again, keep in mind that talking to someone in this way is a privilege. Don't abuse that privilege. People have their own lives and their own concerns. Be respectful of that reality.

• 5. STRENGTHEN YOUR SPIRIT •

No coward soul is mine,
No trembler in the world's storm-troubled sphere:
I see Heaven's glories shine,
And faith shines equal, arming me from fear.
—EMILY BRONTË, "Last Lines"

Whatever your concept of a Higher Power or Great Spirit or God may be, this is a wonderful time to ask for support and assistance from that source. As the twelve-step programs suggest, we are limited in what we can do. Therefore, we need help. And now is the time to ask for it. If the spirit moves you, attend church or synagogue, sit alone in a place of worship, light candles, pray and meditate. Seek spiritual nourishment and assistance in whatever form feels right to you. Find a spiritual practice that works for you, one that allays your fears and helps you get through your day.

One of the primary obstacles many women face when turning to God is that they often picture a judgmental male divinity figure. We must turn away from such an image for the simple reason that it is impractical and too self-limiting for us now. The last thing you need is a judgmental God, though I question whether such a thing really exists.

What I believe women need more than anything else, especially in times of crisis, is mothering. We give so much as mothers and we ask for so little in return. Yet we forget that we need mothering, too. How many of us have attracted an older and wiser woman into our lives who is capable of loving us for who we truly are? That kind of love is rare, in part because we rarely seek it out. We attempt to give mothering without realizing that we need mothering. We serve as mothers—too often to grown men—but we refuse to acknowledge our own need for a mother's love.

Many women respond to this point by saying, "I am too old

to be mothered." I believe we are never too old to be mothered, just as we are never too old to give motherly love, even to those who are well beyond their childhood. Most of us were asked to give motherly love at a very young age. Long before we were mothers ourselves, many of us gave such love to our younger siblings, or even to one or both of our parents. How many of us truly received all the mothering we needed as children, or even as young adults? I have counseled thousands of women, and I can tell you with assurance that most women I have seen have not received enough motherly love to support them in their lives. Even worse, they believe that they no longer deserve that love because they are now twenty-five or thirty-five or forty-five or fifty-five years of age. I am not saying that we should all become needy little children in the presence of older women. Most of us are far too mature and independent for that, anyway. What I *am* saying is that few of us are aware of our need for motherly love and the fact that we need occasional infusions of this love. Sometimes you should drop all your burdens and allow yourself to be loved as a child who has turned to her mother for support.

For those who have had good and loving mothers, this act of surrender may come easier, especially if you have good memories of falling into the arms of your mother. If that is your experience, I urge you to remember how cleansing and supportive such surrender was. Never let that memory go. On the contrary, keep it fresh by being willing to surrender your burdens from time to time. Let all your worries and concerns fall away. Drop out for an evening. Allow your own natural compassion for yourself to come bubbling up to the surface.

No matter how difficult or wonderful your mother may have been, I believe that many of us deny ourselves real compassion even as we struggle valiantly against enormous difficulties. We do this, I believe, because we do not know how to mother ourselves. Instead of giving ourselves the kind of unconditional love and acceptance that a loving mother gives, we criticize ourselves, judge ourselves harshly, and remind ourselves every day of how we are failing. The little voice inside of us is ready and able to tell us how inadequate we are. Rarely is there an inner voice—or an outer manifestation of it—that tells us how proud we are of ourselves, how much we have accomplished, and how far we have come on so little support. Most of us have not contacted that aspect of ourselves that can provide us with nonjudgmental love. The reason we do not have a nurturing, nonjudgmental source of love within ourselves is that we haven't yet contacted the Great Mother archetype within ourselves.

Unfortunately, the mother image that most of us are preoccupied with is the memory of the critical mother who raised us. All mothers draw their inspiration—indeed, their maternal instincts—from the archetypal mother. However, our image of the archetypal mother need not be limited to any one figure, especially to the mother who raised us. We can identify the source of unconditional love and acceptance, the Great Mother within each of us, and begin a relationship with her at any point in our lives. One of the healthiest ways I know of to do this is simply to turn to the Great Mother archetype in meditation and prayer.

All of us can sit and pray to or meditate on the image of the Great Mother. A meditation that can help you do that follows on the next page. This meditation can be a source of daily strength and relief from fear. There are many other ways you can derive strength from spiritual activities. Pray, meditate, read the Bible or other spiritual literature.

Another way to enjoy greater spiritual peace is to take long walks in nature—say, in a forest or at the ocean or in the desert. Whatever allows you to surrender your burdens and feel nourished by some spiritual source is an altogether positive activity and should be engaged in regularly.

Meditation on the Great Mother for Support, Love, and Guidance

Sit alone on a comfortable chair in a quiet place in your home, perhaps your bedroom. Exhale, drop your shoulders, and pay attention to your breath for a few minutes. Allow yourself to sink deeply into a state of relaxation. Continue to pay attention to your breath. Allow yourself to breathe deeply and rhythmically. Once you feel fully relaxed, allow any emotions that might be at the surface of your consciousness to emerge and be felt. Whatever emotion wants to be recognized, allow it to rise before you. Anger, fear, or sadness. Let them all come up.

As these feelings emerge, picture a woman of undeterminable age and limitless love and wisdom come into your presence, as if she has emerged from behind a veil in your consciousness. More than any other characteristic, this woman possesses infinite love for you. She is so glad to see you. She knows that you are in pain and feel alone. She comes to you now to be with you and remind you that you are never alone, that you always have her to help you.

In order for her to speak to you, she uses your voice, but the inspiration for each word comes from her. Using your voice inside your mind, she tells you that she is immensely proud of you. She delights at your courage, honesty, and enormous capacity for love. You have suffered so much in your life, she tells you. Yet despite all that you have been through, you have come so far—much further than anyone might have thought. You are a marvel in her eyes. Her biggest wish is that you would love yourself as much as she loves you; she wishes that you would be as proud of yourself as she is of you. She tells you that she is caring for you and your children and watching over you all every day. She tells you not to be afraid; she is watching over every step you take. Continue to work hard and do all that you are doing in the best spirit possible. She is helping you on your path. Express all your concerns to her. Tell her every bit of fear and grief and sadness you feel. Let it all rush out. Surrender all your pain to her. Let her lead you gently and gradually out of your problems. Relax. She is taking care of everything, your mother.

When you feel you have expressed yourself fully, allow yourself to come out of your reverie.

. . .

• 6. ENJOY GUILTY PLEASURES—WITHOUT THE GUILT •

Another way to escape from fear is to enjoy guilty pleasures—and in today's culture, there are a lot of them.

- *The People's Court.* As I mentioned earlier, I got home early a few days each week and enjoyed watching Judge Wapner bringing sanity and justice to everyday insanity. Oh, how reassuring Judge Wapner was to me. He always seemed to see through the smoke screen people threw up and into the very heart of the matter. As I watched the judge make sense of every sort of petty conflict, I prayed that my own court hearing would be overseen by such a wise figure.
- *The National Enquirer.* What fun to read about the faux pas of celebrities and the latest visits from outer space. After a day of listening to my clients' problems and having to face my own between appointments, I loved nothing better than to curl up with *The National Enquirer*'s latest revelation about celebrities or some woman who is pregnant with a Martian baby.
- *The Love Connection.* Watching men and women choose new partners or fight with old ones gave me vicarious pleasure. Wouldn't life be great if we could go back and choose new partners or have some TV show arrange our next date? Well, maybe not. But it was fun watching others do it. Also, after botching my marriage so thoroughly, I loved watching women and men choose some new dream partner. It was a pleasant alternative to considering my own mess.
- The unholy duo of Howard Stern and Jerry Springer. When I was really feeling down, when I really felt as if I had made a complete mess of my life, I would sometimes tune into Howard Stern or Jerry Springer. My life seemed a lot saner after a half hour with either of these guys.
- Oprah Winfrey, the antidote to Jerry Springer. Oprah runs a nationwide therapy session every day of the week and I love

her for it, as so many millions of other women do. She's wise, strong, funny, and imperfect enough to be real. And somehow she communicates so well with her audience and her guests that we all feel as though we know and love her.

• Feng shui, a Chinese geomantic practice. According to feng shui, our homes represent aspects of our lives and each room in our house represents a particular part of our lives, depending on where that room is located. One room represents our love life, another helpful friends, another our careers, another wealth, and still another fame and fortune. By arranging the furniture in these rooms in just the right way, by placing certain objects, such as crystals in just the right places, we can enhance these areas of our lives, just as we enhance the feeling in these rooms. I was hooked. When I learned about feng shui, it became my new and happiest hobby. I redid my entire house, including my backyard, according to the instructions of a local feng shui artist. I put a flowing fountain in one corner of my yard—the wealth part, of course—and attributed every new good fortune to the way energy moved in my house and my life. Maybe it's superstition or simple craziness, but feng shui gave me great pleasure and a feeling that I could enhance my life by working within my home and myself, rather than having to manipulate events outside myself, which is what I was doing most of the time.

There are countless hobbies and guilty pleasures most of us can enjoy without any harm being done to our minds or hearts. Of course, I encourage you to avoid indulging too much in unhealthy foods or alcohol. On the other hand, enjoy the harmless petty pleasures that people usually look down on, but find themselves sneaking every once in a while.

• A MOTHER NEEDS A MOTHER •

When you actively nurture and care for yourself, you realize that what you are doing is mothering yourself. All the steps I've described in this chapter to reduce fear and get the care you need are actually practical ways to love yourself in a way that a mother would love you. This love is nonjudgmental and comforting. You don't have to be anything special to receive this love. In fact, the more critical you are of yourself, the less you can give yourself the kind of love I have described here.

Being the good mother to yourself can be difficult if your biological mother was critical of you. In fact, engaging in acts of self-love will automatically bring you into a confrontation with the critical mother within you. Simply continue to love yourself in the ways I have described. By doing the practical steps, you are allowing the good mother, the archetypal mother, to overcome the critical, destructive mother. The more you actively love yourself, the more the archetypal mother can come into your life.

The result of this shift is so profound that I cannot begin to describe the kind of effect it can have on you. When you realize that there is a source, perhaps even a divine source, pouring love and life energy into your being, your own capacity to love yourself grows stronger. All that guilt and self-condemnation and those feelings of inferiority start to fade away. You begin to realize that you are a loved human being. But more important, that love is not predicated on someone else but on something that flows within you, unconditionally and without limit.

5 HOW TO PARENT YOUR CHILDREN
DURING THE CUSTODY SUIT

Advising you on how to parent your children during a custody suit is a little like telling you how to prevent a forest fire after starting one yourself. I did some things right but a lot of things wrong. Even after you read this chapter and decide to do the very best job you can, you will no doubt make a lot of mistakes that you've been warned against. Don't despair. Being a parent is the toughest job that anyone can ever do, even when not under the terrible pressures of a custody suit. It's also the least celebrated job.

I'm not sure of all the many factors that make up a good parent, and I am not going to pretend to embody them. I do know that the first and most important one is to love your children with all the love you have. Still, our children reflect not only the love we give them, but the totality of our humanity— that is, our strengths, talents, flaws, and weaknesses. They become people, just as we did. And just as we have had to do, they will have to take the healing path, finding solutions to their internal and external problems. At some point, we must surrender them to that path. We can only do that if we have faith in some higher power that we pray will guide them to their solutions and, most of all, to love. It took a great leap of faith for me to accept and integrate that I both succeeded and failed as a parent and to be at peace with that paradox.

Parenting is not an all-or-nothing endeavor. We all succeed to varying degrees. For example, during the custody suit I tried hard not to talk too much to my children about their father, and I deliberately avoided criticizing him in front of them. Unfortunately, I wasn't perfect. Sometimes I let comments slip and my children, as you will read, were hurt by my remarks.

I did not entirely fail in my efforts, however. I held my tongue; I feigned acceptance; I supported when I felt unsupported; I was understanding even when I was not being understood. And I did all of this more than anyone will ever know. It would be very easy for me—or anyone in this situation—to think of myself as a failure. But that perspective, I found, invites surrender and indulgence in all the wrong behaviors, many of which would have been destructive to my children, to me, and ultimately to my cause.

As I said earlier, you must do your best to honor yourself as a good and loving mother. At the same time, you must do all you can to get the support you need. For the most part, you will not be able to get that support from your children. They will give you their love, which is reward enough. But in the end, you must support them during this time of crisis. That's why I emphasize that you get your needs met, in part so that you can go on being the best mother you can be.

Below I allow my children to tell you about their experience during this time, which was life-altering, to say the least. I believe that by allowing your children to talk about the custody suit, you will better understand its effects on them and therefore better address their needs. To keep my children from feeling inhibited in their remarks, I asked my coauthor, Tom Monte, to interview them without my being there.

To give their thoughts some perspective, allow me to repeat their ages at the time of this interview, as well as when they were going through the custody battle. My oldest son, Rob, was eighteen when the interview was conducted. He was thirteen in 1994 and fourteen in 1995, the years the custody battle took place. Brandon, my middle son, was seventeen when he was interviewed; thirteen and fourteen at the time of the custody suit. Kristina, my daughter, was fifteen when interviewed and ten and eleven during the two years of the suit.

While the suit was under way, I moved the children to Orlando, Florida, as the children note several times in the following interview.

What was your reaction to the news that your mother was being sued for custody by your father?

ROB: It came as a complete surprise to me. I was away with my dad when the sheriff's department came and told my mother that my father was suing for custody. My dad and I had taken a road trip to North Carolina. We were having a good time and nothing was said to me at all. When I got home and heard the news, I didn't know what it was all about. But then it started to dawn on me and it came as a total shock.

BRANDON: We were all in shock.

ROB: Our father seemed like a bad guy at first. He was the one who started the suit.

BRANDON: Taking us to court didn't help. It could have been so much better.

KRISTINA: The person who is going to sue should really think about their reasons. Do they have all the right reasons?

BRANDON: Sometimes it felt like the custody suit was really about my parents trying to get back at each other.

What were the predominant feelings you experienced during the time of the custody suit?

ROB: There was just so much going on at the time. The custody thing, all these feelings, and the demands of school. I was trying to deal with everything at once. It was overwhelming. Also, I didn't want to live in Miami. But there were reasons for not wanting to go back to Miami that had nothing to do with my dad. For one thing, I was getting beat up almost every day in school when I lived in Miami. Life was just bad there. I was skipping school a lot. I wanted something different and to start something new. Moving to Orlando was a new opportunity and a new life.

BRANDON: Most of the time it was confusing. I was younger then and I didn't understand what was going on. I didn't know if we were going to end up with Mom or Dad. I tried to do everything normally, but it was hard because the situation was always on my mind. I wanted to live with Mom. I didn't want things to change. Everything would stay the same if Mom had custody. But it was scary, because I didn't really know what was going to happen.

KRISTINA: I agree. It was hard not knowing what would happen. I wasn't too worried or doubtful about Mom winning. But I tried not to think about Mom losing and having to live with Dad.

BRANDON: When my parents were married, I never thought they would divorce, and when they divorced, I never believed there would be this custody battle, but when it happens, you just have to move through it.

Did you have feelings of disloyalty toward either or both of your parents during the custody suit?

BRANDON: I remember we went to the courthouse one day. I didn't know what it was about. I was just sitting in the waiting room and it was weird. I was sitting between Mom and Dad and I didn't want to talk to either of them because I didn't want one to think that I was siding with the other. And I was just torn between the both of them.

KRISTINA: I had feelings of disloyalty a lot, too. If I went over to my dad's house and talked about my mom, he didn't want to hear it. I couldn't talk about Dad in front of Mom, either.

ROB: I love both my parents, but the choice was to live with my mother. I love my dad. I didn't want to have to take sides or make one seem better than the other.

BRANDON: I felt like if I was getting along with one, I was betraying the other. It seemed like I was never getting along with both of them at the same time.

KRISTINA: Whenever you got both of them together, there was an argument. When we were alone with one of our parents, it sometimes felt like brainwashing, hearing one parent talk bad about the other.

BRANDON: Some of it convinced me and some of it didn't. Some of what I heard changed my whole opinion of what I felt about my mom or dad. Some of it I dismissed.

Were you angry at them?

ROB: I was angry at both my parents. I blew up a few times. I threw stuff around and broke a lot of stuff. I was yelling and screaming, taking it out on the wrong people, being self-destructive. When you're that young, you don't know how to deal with your emotions.

BRANDON: I was angry at both my parents. I couldn't talk to them about it, but I did feel angry at times.

KRISTINA: I was more angry at Dad for suing Mom for custody.

BRANDON: Sometimes it felt like we were pawns, too. Mom would ask us about what we do at Dad's and Dad would ask about Mom and we would be caught in the middle. And after a while, it didn't seem like a custody battle but about them getting at each other and we were caught in the middle.

KRISTINA: Sometimes I felt like I couldn't do anything right. Dad's lawyer was mean. He made my brothers turn around and then made me just talk to him alone.

BRANDON: We called him Jabba the Hut. He was a slimy lawyer. You could tell that all he really cared about was getting his money. He didn't care about the actual dynamics of the case.

You had to see a lot of court-appointed therapists and family service personnel. What effect did they have on you?

ROB: It seemed like we were being pushed around by the therapists. They would ask how we felt about this or that. The only reason they asked us these questions was to show our answers in court. They weren't there to help us. Everything we said about our parents got written down and then was shown in court. I didn't know how we were going to influence the situation. I didn't want to say the wrong thing to the wrong person. Also, there were caseworkers coming in and asking a lot of questions, too. Our emotions were being used in the custody battle, which was really like a war. After a while, we pretty much told them what they wanted to hear.

KRISTINA: Whenever we had to go to see a therapist, I had to be perfect. This got annoying. I had to put on a mask, because I was afraid that if I said the wrong thing, it would hurt my parents and keep us from living with my mother.

ROB: The HRS [family court services] came in and tried to find flaws in our family and tried to nitpick at every little thing. They tried to find flaws in my mother. It was very confusing at the time. I was just a jumble of emotion.

BRANDON: It felt like we were being watched all the time. You can't do anything without it being brought up. Anything that you might say to your dad, he might use it against you or Mom in the future. All our faults were ammunition in court. Dad would find fault with us and use that to show that our mother was being a bad mother. Anything we did wrong—and sometimes I didn't even know we did something wrong—could be used against us and our mother.

KRISTINA: No one was listening to us. This whole thing was quote-unquote about us, but no one was listening to us. You could say that it's something messed up about the legal system, or what people feel about kids. Or both. I don't even know if all the stuff we said to the lawyers or therapists made one bit of difference. I believe that at least 50 percent of the decision should be based on what the kids think.

BRANDON: We were telling lawyer after lawyer, therapist after therapist what we wanted. None of that mattered. It was just up to the court, where no one really even knew us. We couldn't talk to the court.

KRISTINA: People didn't listen to us because we were little kids. The court was going to decide our lives for us, yet they didn't know us.

BRANDON: People don't think that kids have feelings or opinions. They think we were just parroting what the parent you live with was saying.

ROB: It's funny, but no one talked to us about our fears.

How did the custody suit affect your life outside your house?

BRANDON: I felt I was the only one in school going through this. I felt isolated. I still had friends, but I didn't think anyone could relate. It wasn't like a normal carefree school day. It makes your life a lot worse, because you have to worry about who called when you got home. Did a lawyer call? Who got custody? So it makes it hard getting through the day.

KRISTINA: I was in fifth and sixth grade when the custody thing was going on. I didn't make a lot of friends when we moved up here [to Orlando]. I was just going to try to do my work and get on with it.

BRANDON: All of seventh grade, there was that whole thing going on, so I didn't make any real friends, because I was afraid I was going to move back to Miami. But later I made a lot more friends when the ruling came that we could stay in Orlando.

KRISTINA: But afterwards, there was always that feeling that Dad's going to call and it [the custody battle] is going to happen all over again.

What did you do with your anger?

BRANDON: I played a lot of roller hockey. But mostly I bottled it up.

KRISTINA: I was really quiet. I don't know what I did with my emotions.

BRANDON: It's not like we could talk to anyone about what we were feeling. I didn't trust therapists or my mom or dad. I didn't want to talk to my parents about my feelings. I talked a little to my friends about it.

What did your friends say?

BRANDON: My friends just nodded politely. They didn't know what to say. If you haven't gone through it yourself, you can't know how that person is feeling. I couldn't really talk to anyone but my brother and sister. We talked to each other about what was going on.

KRISTINA: I did get closer to my brothers.

BRANDON: You have the situation in common. We all felt the same way about the custody suit. If we lost and went to our dad, we would still all be together. That was comforting. The three of us were more a family than we were with our mother, even. But in the end, the three of us were not going to be broken up and that was comforting.

ROB: Talking to Brandon and Kristina was a comfort to me. We talked about the custody suit a lot. We were the only ones that really understood our situation.

BRANDON: This sort of situation brings out the worst in everyone. Mom would have mood swings. Sometimes I would come home and Mom would be inside crying. We all knew why she was depressed. She'd be fine in the morning. Then when I got back from school, she'd be crying and then she'd get it back together. It seemed like there were cycles.

KRISTINA: Her depression lasted a little bit. I never saw anything like that before, her crying in her room with the door closed.

How did you cope with all of these very powerful feelings?

ROB: I hung out with friends a lot. I listened to a lot of music and played guitar. I didn't talk to many people about what was happening, except to a couple of close friends. I kept my feelings inside. I couldn't talk to people openly.

BRANDON: I tried to study and do everything normally. Sometimes that's the only thing you can do, live your life as normally as possible.

KRISTINA: There was a lot of pressure on us to do well in school. If we had a bad grade or something, it would be brought up that Mom was a bad parent. It just added pressure on us.

BRANDON: I got sick of it. I just wanted to get it over.

KRISTINA: Mom had to write down when Dad called. Sometimes we'd have to tell her what he said and we'd have to pretend to be just happy.

Now that it's over, what effect did the custody battle have on you?

BRANDON: I'm probably a better person for it, I suppose, because I can look back and say that if I got through this, then I can get through a lot of other stuff.

KRISTINA: I'm a lot happier now. It felt like a big weight got lifted off my shoulders. When the judge made the ruling, I said, "Okay, now it's over."

BRANDON: It feels like I missed out on my childhood. As for being in a hurry to grow up, no, I just want to go back and have that time again and be like a normal kid. I want to be like all the other kids.

ROB: After it ended, I was afraid it was going to happen again. Maybe the courts weren't happy about the decision. We were always watching our backs.

What is your relationship like with your parents now?

BRANDON: Now I realize that I can have a separate relationship with my mom and dad. This summer I spent time with my dad in North Carolina and realized I could have a good time with my dad without feeling like I betrayed my mom and vice versa. You just try to take the best qualities of both parents and put the rest behind you. It just happens over time. I think it's like a self-realization—realizing that those problems are my parents' problems. What they feel about each other really doesn't matter. This is the biggest thing I got out of this. What they feel is their problem. It doesn't have to affect the way I feel about either one of them.

KRISTINA: I think you should take the good from each side. When someone bickers about the other one, it will pass. Just get on with your life. We had to grow up fast, though.

ROB: I miss my dad now. I never had much of a relationship with him. We started talking recently, in the last year and a half, and I've gotten to know him better and I feel good about that.

How would you advise parents who are going through a custody suit? How can they better raise their children?

KRISTINA: Listen to your kids.

BRANDON: Don't keep them in the dark about the situation. But also, parents should be careful what they say to their children. They want to vent what's going on and they should think about what they say about the other parent. They shouldn't talk negatively about the other parent. Also, parents shouldn't go over the edge and bring the courtroom into the house. Try not to change the family routines, either. The mother shouldn't start taking drastic measures and change the routine. Also, the family members should be there for each other.

KRISTINA: We knew that they loved us and that wasn't going to change.

BRANDON: The parent who isn't living with the children shouldn't try to come into the kids' lives in such a big way and try to make up for lost time. That happened a lot to us, especially around the holidays. At Christmas, our dad wanted to go out and buy a tree and decorate it with us. It had no meaning to us. It was a little much at the time.

KRISTINA: There was an incident when my dad walked in on a play rehearsal and I just burst into tears and felt all sad and angry because I hadn't seen him in a long time. Parents have to be sensitive to these things. They have to know what their kids are feeling or at least care. They should ask them what they want. They should say, "Do you mind if I come up and decorate the tree or have dinner with you?" It's just assumed that we wouldn't mind.

ROB: Keep talking to your kids. Also, the kids have to listen to both sides, hear what both parents have to say. All we heard was from our mom. Now that I've spoken to my father, it's easier to understand what was going on for him and what his feelings were. I would tell kids to definitely find something that can help you keep your mind off the custody battle. Find someone you can trust and talk to, if you can. If you're living with your mom, definitely spend time with your dad, or vice versa.

KRISTINA: I have a good relationship with my father today. I feel that I learned a lot from the experience of the custody suit and I'm stronger today for it, I believe. But I understand what children go through in this process and I feel for them. I want to help them.

• A MOTHER'S PERSPECTIVE •

Most custody suits take place when the children are young, usually under ten. No matter what their ages, children are driven by three emotions while a custody suit is going on. The first is fear, the second is anger, and the third is their love for both of their parents. Fear and anger drive all the negative behaviors. Their primary fear, of course, is a kind of generalized fear of the future. The questions that make them most afraid include the following: Whom will they live with? Will they lose one or both of their parents? What will their new living situation be like? Will they be blamed by the parent they live with? Many unspoken fears stem from the proceedings themselves. The lawyers, the court-appointed psychologists, the family court services personnel, the judge, and the courtroom itself are all terrifying to children, especially to young adolescents.

The more afraid the children are, the more they will seek to escape through a variety of methods. Some simply stay away from the house, hang out with their friends, watch television endlessly, or play video games. Others turn to drugs. As my children stressed, people have to talk to the kids in a way that communicates how much they care about how the children are feeling. I tried to talk to my children, but in hindsight it wasn't enough.

The truth is, it's hard for a single mother to find the time to talk intimately with her children, but if we are to give them the security they need, we must be very conscious of their needs and find the time.

The second negative emotional state is anger. They will be angry at both of you, but also in conflict over whom to choose. Because you are more available to them—assuming they live with you—and vulnerable, they will likely take out most of their anger, confusion, and frustration on you, their mother. Many children believe that you have betrayed them in some way, because they rely most heavily on you to protect them. How could you let things get this far out of balance? they secretly want to know. How could you allow the family to be destroyed? You already have guilt for your part in your failed marriage. Talk to your children about their feelings. Ask them if they feel betrayed or let down. When they express those feelings, simply say that you are sorry and that you and your former husband did all you could to keep your marriage together, but that sometimes two people are better off apart. Apologize for the custody suit, but avoid blaming your former husband. As you can see from the interview above, the children can figure out for themselves who initiated the suit.

Many children blame themselves for what is happening to the family, even after you and your ex-husband go to great lengths to disabuse them of such feelings. Keep reassuring them that they are not to blame. No doubt they will still be wounded by the divorce itself and will still hold out some faint hope that you and your former husband will get back together. They may even hope that the judge will order the two of you back together.

The key, as my own children expressed, is for you to talk to them honestly and extensively about what is going on in the custody proceedings. But while you are doing that, try as best you can to observe the following recommendations.

• A FEW GENERAL GUIDELINES TO KEEP IN MIND •

To the extent that you are able, do the following:

- Tell them how much you love them and how much their father loves them. Explain that no matter what the judge decides, they will always have both of their parents. They will always see both of you regularly and whenever they truly want to see one or the other. They will also always be together. No one will separate them from each other.

- Insist on regular hours for your children and do your best to maintain order in their lives. Children need order and routine to feel secure. They need to know your daily patterns—when you leave for work and when you are coming home. They must know how they can reach you in an emergency. Their patterns must be adhered to. They have to go to school during the school year; they should be home for meals and should have a curfew in the evenings and a set bedtime. They have to get their homework done. They need structure, especially when so much in their lives seems as if it's falling apart.

- As much as you can, be mild in your comments about your husband. He's your children's father and they are very protective of him and their feelings toward him.

- What you tell your children about the court proceedings depends on how old they are and their level of maturity. That's a judgment call that you must make. But in general, I would advise you to portray the custody suit as a negotiation between you and your former husband, with a judge helping you to decide which parent the children should live with.

- Spend some time with them every week in which you can be with them alone, without the distractions of the rest of your life. Also, as much as you can, try to focus on your child whenever he or she makes a request or asks a question.

One of the most difficult acts of self-discipline that a parent can perform is to focus exclusively on his or her child when the child asks a question or makes a request. The intense pressure that each of us is under acts as a distraction, pulling our attention away from our children, especially when they make a request of us, even a minor one. We tend to respond to such requests by taking care of them as quickly as we can and then by going back to what we were doing or thinking about. But in that moment, either we give of ourselves entirely or we fail to become fully present. We escape into our own inner world and never really show up for our child. We must avoid doing this as much as we can.

Look your children in the eyes and truly listen to them when they speak. Listening is an act of surrender to the moment and to the request the child is making for our attention.

• SOME GENERAL GUIDELINES FOR •
BEHAVIORS TO AVOID

As much as possible, I strongly urge you to avoid the following behaviors.

- Do not under any circumstances attempt to diminish your children's father in their eyes. It's against the law. It will go against you in court. It will hurt your children. And in the end, it will do more harm to your relationship with your children than it ever could have helped.
- Try your best not to confide your fears, anger, or pain to your children. Don't tell them how hurt you are by what is occurring or by what their father is doing in court.
- Don't use them as therapists or priests. Don't ask them for advice or to find out what their father is thinking or planning, especially with regard to the custody suit.
- Don't confess any ambivalence about what is taking place. It will only confuse them further and fuel their hope that you and your ex-husband will get back together.
- Don't make them feel guilty for what is taking place.
- Try not to ingratiate yourself with your children, even if their father is doing this. Parents inevitably try to sell themselves to their kids during a custody proceeding. What the parents do not realize is that this behavior creates insecurities, anger, and

resentment in the children. It also encourages them to use their newfound power to manipulate the parents for all the wrong reasons. Ultimately, it destroys the natural boundaries between parents and children and will give rise to even greater psychological problems later on.

Children often know on some level that they are being fought over. So many of the legal technicalities, the court orders, and the machinations of the various agencies will be lost on them. But they will also know that the entire affair is taking place for their benefit. They will realize that in some sense the process is staged for them. *They are the prize.*

They may use the fact that they are being fought over to play one side against the other—this month choosing your husband as the good guy, the next month choosing you. It's up to you to be consistent in your love and behavior. They may be just testing you and your love. Eventually they will come around.

- Do not allow them to believe that the outcome is in anyone's hands but the judge.
- Don't give up. Many times I was tempted to hand the children over to their father to stop this terrible process and put an end to everyone's pain. If that happens, take a deep breath, exhale, and release the fear and frustration. Do not give up.

Of all the possible dos and don'ts, the three most important are dos: Love your children with all your heart; maintain consistency in your daily life; and talk to them as much as you can. Set aside time to talk to them about their concerns. Let them know how much you care about what they are going through. Talking and listening to them is love in action. It lets them know their feelings count and that you are there for them.

6 HOW TO DEAL WITH YOUR EX-HUSBAND

Some part of you, perhaps only a small part—the part that has an *Addams Family* sensibility—probably enjoys considering all the many ways your former husband might find his way out of your life. Perhaps he could be run over by a train—purely by accident, of course—or dropped from a great height into shark-infested waters or used as a target at the local firing range. Perhaps he could save everyone a lot of trouble and finally have that long-overdue heart attack—the fatal one. One of my favorite fantasies during my custody battle was that my father was a Mafia don who had the power to simply make my former husband disappear. Ah, the joys the imagination can bring. Yes, whiling away the hours contemplating your former husband's demise has its satisfactions, and even its therapeutic value, but it will not help you deal effectively with him. On the contrary, blind hatred or terrible disappointment will only get in the way. It will prevent you from acting rationally, especially in highly charged moments when your children, good judgment, and pride are at stake. What you really need—even more than a fiendish form of torture—is a strategy for dealing with him when you speak on the telephone or when he picks up the children or when you see him in court.

The first step at arriving at such a strategy is to achieve clarity. Your emotions are dangerous now, especially when they come to the surface in your interactions with him. The mistakes you make can be extremely costly. It's time to look at this thing as coolly and as rationally as you can.

• THE CHILDREN: THE ONLY SUBJECT OVER WHICH •
YOU MUST INTERACT

A custody suit will very likely be the most surreal experience you will ever have. Your former husband is attempting to take away your children—an act of war by anyone's definition. Yet during this war, you and your former husband will be forced to interact from time to time. You will be forced to behave with civility, primarily because the law demands it and because your children need you to behave sanely. With any luck such interactions will be few, but they will occur nonetheless.

The situation gets even more surreal when you consider that your children have ensured that you and your former husband are irrevocably, if loosely, bound together for the rest of your lives. Fortunately, your children are the only part of life over which the two of you need to interact. In most cases, you will communicate with your former husband only through your respective attorneys. But there will be occasions when you will have to deal with him directly—not only during the custody battle but after its resolution.

During my own custody suit, I interacted with my former husband as little as I could. In most cases, my oldest son, Rob, could arrange meetings with his father for himself and his brother and sister. Nevertheless, I still saw my former husband periodically, such as when he came to pick up the children at my house. (I always made sure that the children were waiting for him so that the interaction between us was minimal. Once they were all outside, however, I took a photograph of the four of them as they walked together toward his car or stood outside my house.) I also had to talk to him over the phone and write to him occasionally when something of importance involving the children arose.

The question is, How should you behave when the two of you are within shouting distance of each other? The answer, very simply, is with cool detachment. Pull back and focus exclusively on the facts that revolve around your children. Try visualizing a psychic wall between the two of you; see yourself as addressing him from behind that wall. Speak in a neutral voice. Pretend you are dealing with a colleague at work, someone you are not at all fond of. Limit the amount of time you engage in any discussion to no more than fifteen minutes. Preferably, all interactions, even those that take place over the phone, should be even shorter than that.

Keep in mind that any emotional displays will get you into trouble. If you're lucky, they'll only embarrass you; if you're not, they may jeopardize your suit. The truth is, until the custody suit is over and the dust settles, your relationship is prescribed exclusively by the law. And the law is very strict about such matters.

A father is allowed regular and frequent visitation with his children. Any effort you make to obstruct that relationship is against the law and, if proven, will cost you the custody of your children. Remember that the judge will decide who gets custody of the children based in part on which of you is more likely to promote the relationship between the children and the noncustodial parent. If the judge perceives that you are the more compliant parent, he or she will lean heavily in your favor.

Also keep in mind that a father's relationship with his children—and theirs with him—is sacred and essential to the children's long-term health. That relationship must be honored and supported. Even if he has been distant with them or is a selfish man, your children need him, especially when they are young. Ironically, their need for time with him may be even greater if he has been a less-than-stellar dad. Why? Because most children love their father, regardless of the kind of man he is, and desperately want to be loved by him. If he has not provided that love, the children need to know that he *chose* not to love or was unable to love, not that there was some inherent flaw in them.

Children need a complete sense of family, even if it is a divided one. They need the company of their father. They also need to understand their dad, if they ever hope to understand themselves. For all of these reasons, they need time with him.

Your children want you to be supportive of their relationship with their father; they want to know that your love for them is secure even when they love him. They don't want to feel torn between the two of you and they don't want to have to choose. In the end, they want to know that every time they are with their father, they have your blessing.

As my own children reported in Chapter 5, your children may feel that they must choose between the two of you. They may also feel that they are betraying one parent by being good to the other. Perhaps you will do a better job than I did at promoting their relationship with their father and preventing them from feeling such guilt. The more you encourage them to see their father, the more they will understand that their relationship with him doesn't threaten you. When they realize that, they will know that they are not betraying you by loving him.

The only exception to all that I have said, of course, is if your former husband has been abusive to his children, either verbally or physically. If there is proof of such behavior, then he will lose all custody and unsupervised visitation rights until the children are adults, at which point they can make their own choices. If there is no provable, overt abuse, you are bound by law to support the children's relationship with their father.

Still, you will want to minimize any contact you have with your children's father. In most cases, you can limit your interactions to a brief discussion, either over the telephone or in person, or better yet, in a letter. Here are the primary subjects over which you will be interacting with your former husband while the two of you are fighting over custody, along with my advice on how to limit those interactions.

- Visitation. He will have to come to your home to pick up the children, and you will have to drop off the children so that they can visit him. This may require an occasional brief interaction and a telephone call or two in order to schedule visitation. Of course, have your children ready when he comes. This accomplishes two goals. First, it gets them all out of the house quickly without your having to interact with him at all. Second, it keeps him from snooping around the house. All you need is for him to find something that he can use against you in court. Remember to take a photograph with your date-registering camera whenever he comes to your house or whenever you bring your children to his.

- Their schoolwork and progress. In most cases, you can do this by letter. Meetings with teachers and school administrators will require his presence, either with you or in separate meetings. Choose separate meetings, of course, but keep him informed of everything. He will use it against you in court if you fail to keep him informed. Keep in mind that schoolwork is an area in which you are vulnerable to criticism from him and by court-appointed psychologists. Do your best to help your children keep their grades up, especially during the custody suit. It's not fair that you should be judged harshly by any drop in their grades, but it often happens.

- Their social life, especially if there is a problem to which he should be alerted. Again, a letter is usually all that's needed.

- Their health, especially if a health problem arises. He should be informed of even small changes in his children's health, such as a cold, an ear infection, or a dental concern. These issues can be addressed by letter or e-mail in most cases. Serious health issues require an immediate telephone call. Often health issues, even minor ones, will affect visitation. This usually requires a telephone call as well.

- Financial needs that may exceed your income or child support payments. The best way to communicate such needs is by letter. You can put down your thoughts rationally and document the specific need. Just as money triggered intense emotions during your marriage, it can be an even more sensitive issue after divorce. I strongly urge you *not* to talk about such issues over the phone or in person.

- Special events or behavioral issues that arise unexpectedly. Special events can usually be handled by mail; meetings with teachers or school counselors or administrators may require a telephone call to your former husband, especially if the meeting comes at short notice. Again, it is better to meet separately with teachers and staff than to go together. On the other hand, your former husband may start probing teachers or administrators for information about your children that will reflect poorly on you. If that happens once or twice, you will probably want to stop meeting separately. Your presence may be enough to stop him from looking for trouble.

The only other area that may require interaction with your former husband is if he calls to make an offer to compromise and settle your custody suit. If he makes such an offer, I urge you to politely thank him and tell him that you need time to think the offer over. Do not discuss its substance over the phone, for the simple reason that the situation can easily devolve into an emotional shouting match. Once you have told him that you need time to consider the offer, hang up and get in touch with your lawyer, with whom you should discuss the details.

• THE ODD MAN OUT •

As long as you have custodial care of the children—and you will do everything in your power to keep it that way—your former husband is an outsider to them. This is an extremely awkward position for him to be in, especially if he loves them. For one thing, he very likely suffers from considerable guilt about the divorce and even more about the custody battle. In an odd and twisted way, that guilt may be one of the reasons he is suing you for custody: He may feel he has failed as a father and husband and may now be grasping at ways to restore his place in his children's lives. I do not for a minute believe that such guilt justifies his suit. Nor do I believe that the suit will remedy anything for him or his children, even if he wins. The truth is, his actions are shortsighted, selfish, and in many cases, mean-spirited; they will actually hurt his children and his relationship with them more than if he did nothing at all. Of course you can't tell him or the children that—you must leave it to him to figure that out, or allow your lawyer to make it clear to him if he can't deduce it himself. But the fact remains that he is the person outside the new family, the one created by your children and you. And he's going to be acutely aware of his place outside that bubble. As my son Brandon said in the last chapter, these feelings are going to encourage him to try to make up for lost time, which only makes his relationship with the children more strained.

If you play on his position as an outsider to deliberately weaken his relationship with his children, your children will recognize your behavior and resent you for it. Such actions will increase their sympathy for their father; it will drive them toward him and away from you. Sooner or later, they will see you as a villain.

For many men, being the outsider stimulates anger, resentment, jealousy, and a desire for revenge, feelings that can cause them to harden their positions and insist all the more on custody.

From your point of view, therefore, such feelings are counterproductive, particularly to your hope that the two of you might yet find your way to a settlement. Therefore, I encourage you, as part of your strategy for success, to let your husband know that you want him to spend time with his children.

• DANGEROUS PATTERNS AND THE •
DECISIONS YOU MAKE

Establishing a new behavior pattern with a person who knows you so intimately can be very difficult and sometimes confusing. Creating and maintaining that new relationship requires courage and commitment. You must want to have a new relationship—or, more accurately, to have no real relationship at all. That is extremely difficult for many women and men. For months and even years after your divorce, and even in the throes of a difficult custody battle, people want to fall back into familiar patterns with each other.

All relationships are defined by their patterns. One person is dominant or aggressive, the other recessive or passive; one person more extroverted, the other more introverted; one more controlling, the other more compliant. Though we tend to take turns at these roles, it's also true that all of us are more comfortable in one role or the other. Hence, we fall into patterns.

In marriage, these patterns are particularly strong and apparent. Oddly, even though you are now divorced and being represented by a lawyer, presumably a strong person, you can still easily fall back into the old pattern. If you were passive or easily threatened by your former husband's power, you may find yourself capitulating to his demands, even when you know they do not work for you. He may agree to give you custody if you take less in child support or relinquish some valuable material possession, such as your share of the house. You may argue with your attorney that your former husband's terms must be accepted because he will hold out indefinitely and the legal and emotional costs will become too high to bear. You may make this argument before you have considered the ramifications of his offer on your life. He may be offering less than you and the children need to live. Or he may be holding a valuable possession over your head in order to bully you into accepting an offer that is inherently unfair. Your old behavior patterns can very easily get you into trouble now.

The opposite may be true. You may have been dominant; he may have been passive. In this case, you may have become dissatisfied with his passivity, his withdrawal from life, and the constant need for you to make decisions for both of you. He may be willing to work out a perfectly fair compromise that will allow you to escape this custody suit and avoid a court battle. If you were the more dominant figure in the marriage, you may be used to dismissing his suggestions. Now you must weigh everything he says very carefully to discover the merits of his suggestions.

During my own custody battle, I observed the pattern that had been established between my former husband and me. He clearly was the dominant figure, while I was the passive one. There were many days, weeks, and even months when I was convinced that because of my former husband's determination and strength, he would convince a judge of his competence and my incompetence. This belief alone determined to a great extent the quality of my life during the custody suit. For many months I expected to lose, because I had grown used to losing in our marriage. I was not yet in touch with my own strength. Somehow I had to stand up for what I believed to be right, no matter what.

And then at a crucial moment in the custody suit process, my former husband informed me through our attorneys that he would drop his suit if I agreed to pay him a substantial amount of money. That was a turning point for me. Was all of this just about money? I asked myself. No. I knew he loved his children. There was something else going on here. And then it dawned on me: He had begun to doubt his case and his ability to win this suit. While I had been persevering—and bemoaning my insignificance—his own resolve had been wearing away. And now he hoped to bully me into giving him money before a judge ruled against him.

Even though I realized that his resolve was starting to crack, I still doubted that the judge would rule in my favor. After all, I am a woman who suffered from bulimia. That was my weak point. I considered my former husband's offer long and hard but finally said no, I would not be bullied into giving him money so that I could retain custodial care of my children. I would have to face my past and appear before the court, if that's how far he wanted to take things.

For weeks after I informed my former husband through our attorneys that I would not accept his offer, I was fuming mad. Even if he had followed up his demand for money with a fair offer, I probably would have thrown it back in his face, I was so angry. That would have been a mistake. I never got a chance to do that, however, because he never made a follow-up offer. We were now committed to going all the way to court. Which meant that a lot of trouble still lay ahead.

7 HOW TO DEAL WITH COURT-APPOINTED INVESTIGATORS

Once your case is submitted to the court and is placed on the docket, the investigations into your lifestyle and psychological status begin. You, your former husband, and your children will all be examined and psychologically probed for every possible imbalance or deviant behavior. Believe me, it's worse than the proverbial deep cavity search. A social worker or psychologist from the family court services will show up at your house to investigate the conditions you and your children live under. He or she will interview your children's teachers, school counselors, physician, dentist, and friends, and may even talk to your neighbors. The same will happen to your former husband. Next, you, your children, and your former husband will undergo psychological evaluation by at least one court-appointed psychologist. More than one specialist may get involved, especially if your husband claims that you are mentally unfit to raise your children. In that case, your husband may have his own psychologist evaluate you and your children. All of this can amount to numerous interviews (interrogations might be a better word). In my own case, my children were interviewed by a psychologist four times. From there, the court may order psychological testing for your entire family. Each test can take two or more hours. Finally, the judge can demand that the records of all the psychotherapists you have seen be opened to the court. All your conversations with this person (or persons)—the ones that you believed were confidential and protected by law—can be subpoenaed and thereby become part of the public record for anyone to read. With that, your right to privacy is gone.

Once the investigations, interviews, and testing are concluded, the social workers and the court-appointed psychologists file their reports, including their recommendations as to which of you is better suited to receive custodial care of your children. As you wait for their reports, you lie awake at night wondering if you are still living in the land of the free and home of the brave. And then you realize that you are all on trial to determine if you are a worthwhile mother.

In hindsight, I realize that the reason I was a lamb led to the slaughter was simply that I was unprepared for what happened. All I had was the hope that it would go well. Needless to say, that's not enough. No one had informed me of the dangers inherent in my confrontation with the family court services and the psychologists. I didn't know the rules.

• THE RULES •

Before I tell you the questions you will be asked and what part of your life will be evaluated by the social worker and psychologist, let me tell you how to approach both of these investigations. You should observe certain rules of conduct while being questioned by the social worker and the psychologist. These rules are your safety net. Even if the social worker or psychologist becomes hostile or aggressive, stick to the rules and you'll find your way safely out of a difficult situation.

First, accept that everything you say will be recorded and reported to the court. Nothing is confidential; nothing is off the record, even if you make such a request.

Above all else, be honest, direct, and succinct in your answers. Stick to the question and answer it as briefly as you can. Be specific and cite facts rather than express generalizations. Naturally you should not volunteer any information about yourself that might hurt your chances for retaining custodial care of your children. However, when difficult questions emerge, answer them honestly and succinctly. If you battled some illness that may have a bearing on your case—as was the case for me with my bulimia—give only the basic facts. If the problem has been overcome, report that fact and state that it no longer influences your life or your children's lives.

If you have had a love affair, with either a man or a woman, and are asked about such a relationship, provide only the facts regarding the current status of the relationship. State whether you are still involved with this person or you are no longer involved. Most important, emphasize that your relationship in no way influences the lives of your children. Be very clear that your sexual relationships are private, that you do not bring your lover home with you, and that your children are not privy to the facts of your relationship. State also that you do not have parties at your house, that you rarely bring friends home, and that you maintain regular hours. If appropriate, show the investigator your calendar and point out the stability of your schedule.

Be respectful and sincere without being obsequious. Don't try to elicit sympathy. Do not try to persuade or convince the social worker or psychologist to see your point of view, especially over that of your former husband. These people are not your friends. They do not care about you in any personal way. They have a job to do. That's the extent of their involvement. If the social worker or psychologist exhibits any friendliness or even sympathy, back off. Be wary. It may be their way to loosen your tongue and get you to say things that you may later regret.

When you are asked about your former husband, be understated. Express the positive and the negative in an unemotional, detached way. Answer direct questions with direct answers. If you say something negative about your former husband, do it in a balanced way and then follow your statement up with a specific example or event. Be brief in all your answers regarding your former husband. Do not go on about his faults as a human being. Do not suggest that he has physically or sexually abused you or the children unless you have specific proof.

When asked about your children, stress the positive and keep your answers focused on them. When questioned about them, state your children's dreams and ambitions. Talk about their talents and abilities. Again, follow up generalizations with specifics. When asked about their performance at school, give general grade range. Use your documentation (as described in Chapter 3) to demonstrate your knowledge of their lives. Don't be afraid to be proud of them, but don't overdo it, either.

Don't let questions about your children stimulate you to criticize your former husband.

When asked with whom your children want to live, answer directly and succinctly. Elaborate only if you are asked to explain. You can always encourage the social worker or the psychologist to ask your children for themselves.

Many court-appointed psychologists attempt to achieve some kind of settlement between you and your former husband so as to spare everyone the trauma of having to go to court. When asked about your demands, be clear, specific, and direct. Express your flexibility on certain issues and state specifically where you would be willing to compromise. Do not imply that you would surrender custodial care, however, unless that is your wish.

State the kind of visitation schedule you wish to establish with your former husband, whether it be a flexible visitation or a structured one (both are described in Chapter 1).

Very important: *Demonstrate compliance.* While you are being interviewed, keep in mind that the social worker, the psychologist, and the court are all looking for the parent who will be most compliant with the court order, thereby ensuring that the noncustodial parent will be able to visit his or her children unencumbered by the custodial parent. Compliance, therefore, is a big factor in your favor.

Do not call the social worker or psychologist after you have been interviewed unless you have been specifically instructed to do so.

• KNOW THE TEST QUESTIONS IN ADVANCE •

Both you and your former husband will be investigated in order to determine where the best interests of the children lie. The question is whether the children's best interests are served by turning custodial care over to you or to your former husband. To determine this, a social worker from the family court services will come to your home and conduct a thorough investigation of your life and your children's, evaluating you in several areas. Here are the most important of these:

YOUR HOME

The social worker will evaluate your home for its location within the community, its proximity to schools, churches, day care, and medical facilities. You do not have to be particularly close to any of these services and institutions. You just shouldn't be too far away, such as deep in the woods with little access to a school, a hospital, or day care (especially if you work full-time).

Your home will be inspected to determine if it is sanitary and if all the utilities are working. The social worker will also check to see if your children have enough room. When I lived in Miami, my two boys shared a room and my daughter had her own room. That was fine. In the end, as long as the house is not crowded, it is clean and well ordered, and the utilities work, it will pass inspection.

YOUR RELATIONSHIPS

Technically, your relationships are not supposed to matter, but they do, especially since you can be disqualified on the basis of immorality. Be sure that you do not expose your children to any relationship that might be construed by a hostile investigator as exposing your children to immorality. Do not allow a boyfriend to sleep over at your house and be sure to be home at night. Your children should not know anything about your sex life. Indeed, as far as they are concerned, you don't have one.

YOUR SCHEDULE

The question that is being asked regarding your schedule is this: Are you available enough to your children to actually parent them? Having to work full-time does not disqualify either you or your husband. Emphasize that you are available by telephone at any time at your office and that you can get away if your children need you. If you travel or are away on business a lot, it counts against you. Emphasize that you compensate for your travel by being home for long stretches of time and are available to your children at a moment's notice when you are at your office.

YOUR CHILDREN'S PREFERENCES

Your children's preferences as to which parent they live with is a significant factor, but as I have said elsewhere, it is not the sole determinant. What your children want is only one of many other important factors. Unfortunately, in many cases, judges, social workers, and psychologists believe that the children are parroting one or the other of their parents. Therefore, the children's preferences are often considered to be less important, especially if the court is leaning away from the parent with whom the children want to live.

THE STATUS QUO

If you already have custodial care of your children, it counts strongly in your favor because the court is reluctant to disrupt the children's lives. The old saying that possession is nine-tenths of the law has a certain amount of truth to it, though it does not even approach nine-tenths.

PSYCHOLOGICAL BACKGROUND

People who strive for health are usually the ones who see psychotherapists, while those who are ill and dangerous usually avoid therapy. Unfortunately, courts don't see it that way. Lawyers will use the fact that a woman has seen a therapist as proof of her instability. Also, family court services will question you on all forms of counseling that you have sought. Therefore, when asked by the court and court services, relate all your therapy to particular times in your life when you were under stress. Be prepared to explain the circumstances. Be specific as to the details and the kinds of issues you were facing at the time. Make it clear that the therapy was intended to help you get through a particularly difficult period or that it was marital counseling. When that time was over, you no longer needed the therapy and it was concluded.

• WHAT YOU WILL BE ASKED BY THE PSYCHOLOGIST •

During your interview with the psychologist, he or she will ask you a number of questions to gauge how active and present you are in your children's lives. You must answer every one of these questions thoroughly. The fact that you are documenting your life and your children's (as described in Chapter 3) will be extremely helpful to you in your interview. Bring your three-ring binder with the pouches and refer to it whenever necessary to demonstrate your knowledge of your children and your deep involvement in their lives.

Here are some of the most important questions you will be asked.

- What are your children's interests? Detail the interests of each of your children.
- How are they progressing in school? Document your points with specific grades and any comments from teachers.
- Who helps them with their homework? Report the time of the day your children typically do their homework and when you usually help them. Give specifics whenever possible.
- Who are your children's teachers?
- Who enrolls them in extracurricular activities? Give the specific activities each child is engaged in.
- Are your children involved in any sports?
- Who are your children's coaches and extracurricular instructors?
- Who are your children's school counselors?
- Are your children involved in any special educational or remedial learning programs?
- What activities do you share with your children? These may include watching them at their sporting events; escorting them to their music lessons; going out to eat or to the movies together; taking walks; taking trips or vacations with them; serving as an escort for their school field trips; helping them with their school projects; attending religious services together.
- Who purchases your children's clothing?
- Who takes them to their doctor and dentist appointments?
- Who prepares their meals?
- What do your children like to eat? To wear? To read?
- Who takes them to school in the morning or to the bus stop?
- Who helps them resolve their problems? Without compromising your child's privacy, offer specifics here.
- Who shares their triumphs? Again, cite specific examples.
- Who taught your children to walk? Talk? Read? Count? Who toilet-trained them?
- What is your children's school schedule?

- What are their weekend schedules?
- What is your weekday schedule?
- What is your weekend schedule?
- What is your social schedule?
- What is your travel schedule?
- Who are your children's babysitters?
- Who are your children's neighborhood friends?
- Do you have pets?
- Do the children have grandparents? If so, how close do they live? How involved are they in your children's lives?
- Do your children have a stepparent?
- If so, what is their relationship with him or her?
- Do your children have half-siblings?
- If so, what is their relationship with them?
- Are your children on any medications?

Finally, at some point in the interview, you will be asked about yourself as a parent, about your former husband's strengths and weaknesses as a parent, and about your marriage in general. Likely questions include the following:

- What are your strengths as a parent?
- What are your weaknesses?
- What are the strengths and weaknesses of the other parent?
- Tell me about your marriage.
- How will the other parent answer that question about you?
- Which parent do your children prefer to live with?
- What motivates their preference?

The best way to answer these questions is to tell the truth as objectively and as dispassionately as possible. First and foremost, never say anything about yourself or your former husband that isn't true or that can't be substantiated. If you believe that your former husband is a good parent, have the courage to say that. Such a response will very likely cast you in a positive light, since it reveals your objectivity and your ultimate concern for the health and well-being of your children. It also demonstrates that you know what a good parent is and that you value that above the conflicts that have emerged in your marriage and in the custody suit. Many of us have marital skills that don't work but parenting skills that do. On the other hand, if your former husband was a poor parent, report that and then support that assertion with facts. As you relay this information, do it with as little emotion as possible. A psychologist who sees you lose control of your emotions might decide that you lose your temper too easily, not only with your former husband but with your children. You also appear to lack any degree of objectivity. Remember, you are attempting to convince others of your maturity, equilibrium, and competence as a parent. You are not trying your case against your husband in the psychologist's office.

Do not attempt to curry favor with the psychologist. Such behavior will also go against you. You are not there to sell yourself. This is not a popularity contest. You are the best parent for your children. Let the facts reveal and support that basic truth.

• DON'T BE AFRAID OF THE DARK •

Telling the truth about your darkest secrets, the things only your former husband knows and is now using to take your children from you, can be terrifying. At least it was for me. What makes the experience even worse is that it is not limited to a single admission. You must state again and again to a battery of social workers, psychologists, and lawyers that you had an illness or you engaged in some other behavior potentially damaging to your court case.

No one could convince me that his or her secrets were more inflammatory and dangerous than my own. Bulimia is a disorder practiced in secret. I remember times when I was utterly possessed by the illness, as if it were a demon that rode on my back. Now the investigators were coming to ferret out my secrets and use them against me. Oh, how I feared this next phase of the custody process. Initially, I envisioned my inquisitors as jackbooted gestapo agents who would come into my home and rifle through my cabinets and ask me a lot of personal questions. I would be summoned to their offices for more interrogations until they finally wrenched from me even those secrets I didn't know I kept.

No, I told myself before the process began. I will not go into this process thinking the worst of all these people. And then one day a woman called and introduced herself as a social worker for the family court services. She needed to interview me for my custody case, she said. We agreed on a day and time to meet. Apparently, she would see me after she saw my former husband. In other words, she would be armed and dangerous.

Finally, at the appointed hour, the social worker arrived, pulling into my driveway in a red Mercedes-Benz—brand new, as far as I could make out. My, social workers must be doing well, I told myself. Out stepped an attractive young woman dressed in a beige designer pantsuit. I greeted her at the door and showed her into my living room, where I had intended to sit with her and allow her to conduct the interview. When I suggested she sit down, she refused. "I have to look at the house," she said in a cool, detached voice. She was not going to be charmed by me, her tone informed me.

"Of course," I said. As we went from room to room, she said nothing. Instead, she buried herself in a legal-size notebook attached to a clipboard. She wrote in such a way as to create a shield around herself that kept me at a distance. Her note-taking got fast and furious when we went through the children's rooms. She marched imperiously from room to room as if conducting a military inspection. Her whole manner indicated that she was in charge.

Under most circumstances, I was proud of my house. The interview took place before we moved to Orlando, and at the time, I lived in a recently built, stylish home on the edge of a beautiful golf course. Needless to say, on the day my inquisitor arrived, the house was immaculate. Even the children's rooms were neat and clean, which is more than I could say for most other days. Still, the social worker's icy demeanor and the air of hostility that surrounded her made this tour of my house torturous. I became increasingly self-conscious. Suddenly I started noticing things that were out of place, areas of the house that needed maintenance, even a spot or two that made me draw back in horror. I knew she saw it all; in fact, it seemed to me that the house's flaws were all she saw.

Finally the inspection was over. We went back to the living room and I sat down. Still standing, the social worker cast a critical eye around the room, again with that same imperious air, placed her hand on her hip, looked me dead in the eye, and said, "So. I hear that you don't cook. Is that because of your eating disorder?"

As much as I had been prepared to deal with that issue, the way she asked me threw me momentarily into shock. For a minute, I didn't know what to say. I remember thinking that her attack reminded me of that old loaded question "When did you stop beating your wife?" Even before I answered her question, I was already indicted.

For some reason, my gaze went down to the floor. It was then that I noticed that she was wearing black combat boots. I studied them for a moment. All my worst fears had come true, I realized.

"Yes," I said. "I don't cook mostly because of my eating disorder." I had already been on the defensive with the inspection of my home, but now I was down for a mandatory eight count.

From there the questions started flying.

"Why do you think this is a better environment to raise your children than your ex-husband's home?"

"What makes you think that you would be a better parent to your children than your ex-husband?"

"What are your strengths and weaknesses as a parent?"

"What are your husband's?"

As I mentioned in Chapter 1, I was forced to change attorneys early in the custody process. At the time of this interview, I was still with my first attorney, who had advised me that when I was asked about my ex-husband's faults as a parent and a spouse, I should have let loose with my criticisms of him. This was a big mistake. I didn't realize it at the time, but any question about your ex-husband is a trap. Essentially, it is an invitation to be a bitch. What I should have said was simply: "I prefer not to list my former husband's faults. You can talk to the children about their perceptions of him and me." At the very least, I should have listed one or two of my perceptions in a detached manner. Instead, I followed my attorney's advice and essentially fell into the trap.

I proceeded to briefly list my former husband's strengths as a person and a parent, and then described at length our problems as a couple and his shortcomings as a father. To my horror, the social worker started to make comments that appeared to defend my former husband. Now she seemed even more critical of me. I was already on the defensive, but now I found myself backpedaling and wishing I had said nothing at all about him. In fact, I was wishing I had somewhere safe to hide.

Finally she stood up. "I want the names of every psychotherapist you have ever seen," she demanded.

"I thought that was protected information," I said.

"The court can order this information and I am requesting it now."

Fearing that I would appear resistant and therefore hiding

something—in fact, the worst was already out in the open—I told her that I would get her the names of my former therapists. With that, the interview was over. As I closed the door behind her, I felt myself go numb and weak in the knees. I collapsed on my couch and cried for half an hour. For the rest of the day, I was shell-shocked.

As fate would have it, I had previously agreed to have a friend give a presentation on Amway to a small group of people at my home that same night. That evening, a little group gathered in my living room and chatted away about soaps, bathroom cleansers, and kitchen supplies. Meanwhile, I meditated darkly on what life would be like without my children.

• THE REPORTS COME BACK •

After numerous discussions with the social worker and the psychologist and then an extensive battery of tests, I waited anxiously for the three reports—the social worker's, the psychologist's, and the testing results. Both the social worker and psychologist would make recommendations to the court as to whom the children should live with. Of course, I envisioned the worst. In fact, the report was more favorable than I dared allow myself to hope.

The social worker made the following recommendations:

Should parental responsibility be shared?	**Yes**
Who should be the residential parent?	**Mother**
Who should be the nonresidential parent?	**Father**

The reasons she gave are illustrative of women battling for custody of their children. "There does not seem to be any doubt that both parents love their children and that each parent plays an essential role in their children's psychological development," the report stated. "This consultant is recommending that Ms. Hunter remain as the primary residential parent. Ms. Hunter has been the primary residential parent since 1991 and to make a change in the children's living situation at this time would not be in their best interest."

As I stated elsewhere, possession of the children carries a great deal of weight, especially because moving the children is often considered highly disruptive to their lives and therefore not in their best interests.

Still, despite her recommendation, the social worker could not help taking a few swipes at me. She reported that I had been "in and out of psychotherapy since 1962." She also suggested it would be unlikely that I would follow the visitation agreement that allowed my former husband to see our children on the weekends because I would have to drive four and a half hours from Orlando to Miami to ensure that the children saw their father. But as I told the social worker when she interviewed me, I had a thriving therapy practice in Miami and had to go there on weekends in order to earn my living. In fact, I would maintain that practice for the next two years.

The psychologist's report was far more supportive of me, however. His recommendations were as follows:

1. That Ms. Hunter be awarded primary residential custody of the children in the Orlando area, subject to the children having reasonable visitation with their father.
2. That every and all opportunities be made available for the father to visit his children.
3. Upon the court's determination of primary residential custody, that the parties be directed to family mediation to work out the visitation agreement.
4. As previously mentioned, that the father and Ms. Hunter be directed to participate in co-parenting and/or postmarital

counseling. Family court services can assist the court with a qualified postdivorce counselor.

5. That family court services continue to monitor the progress of this case.

Finally the psychological testing results came back. The report spoke for itself. "Ms. Hunter produced a valid MMPI suggesting open and honest responses, the absence of severe psychological pain, and feeling the ability to cope with the demands of life. None of the clinical scales evidenced significant elevation, offering little opportunity for interpretation or indication of psychopathology."

I felt a deep sense of satisfaction, particularly from the test results, because they assured me that no matter what my former husband threw at me in court, I would have something to fall back on to demonstrate my mental health. But even more personally, the psychologist's report and test results demonstrated that despite my history of an eating disorder, I had regained my health.

I had won the first round, small as that victory was. Still, any satisfaction that these reports gave me was fleeting. Only the judge's decision mattered. It was clear to me now that everything rested on how well I presented myself in court.

8 HOW TO SUCCESSFULLY PRESENT YOURSELF BEFORE THE COURT

Going to court and facing a judge in a custody suit is like going before a king or queen you know nothing about and having that person decide the fate of your children. Is he or she benevolent and wise, as you hope, or is the monarch a tyrant? How should I behave in front of such a person? you ask yourself. How should I dress? How do I communicate that I should be the one to raise these children, without appearing obsequious or full of false pride? How do I win the judge's favor?

These are some of the questions you ask yourself as you prepare to go to court. Unfortunately, unless you have a coach to guide you or you read this book before going to court, you may not arrive at the right answers to these very important questions. Certainly I didn't. In fact, I made virtually every mistake I could possibly make. I dressed inappropriately and presented myself in all the wrong ways. I didn't know it until much later, but my choices were motivated by all the wrong images and impulses. Had I had the benefit of a coach or someone who could have helped me think through what I was experiencing, I would not have made the same mistakes. But hindsight is always twenty-twenty, as they say. I offer my experience as an illustration of what *not* to do when you go to court.

My case was ordered to the Eleventh Judicial Circuit Court of Dade County, Florida. In all, we made five appearances before the court. The first, which occurred in July 1995, nearly a year after I was served the custody papers, was held to determine if I could legally move my children to Orlando, some two hundred miles to the north of Miami. That hearing lasted only an hour, during which time I was granted temporary permission to move. Our second appearance was scheduled for early August 1995, but had to be postponed because the judge got sick and canceled at the last minute. The next appointment, the guardian ad litem canceled at the last minute. A few days later, on a Sunday in late August of 1995, we had our first all-day session. It ran from 9 in the morning to 8 at night.

My former husband, who is a uniformed civil servant, wore his dress uniform. His costume made a very striking and obvious statement: This is a man who has served his community and country.

I wore a high-collared black two-piece outfit, a skirt and jacket with a very subtle brown print from Ann Taylor. I had on dark stockings, black shoes, and pearls. I had my hair styled and I had applied some makeup—not heavy, but visible. In other words, I was a walking disaster. I wanted to communicate that I was responsible and elegant and that I had a take-charge personality.

The source of my choices was not an inner knowledge of my true identity or any deep thinking about my circumstances, but an image that was irrelevant to the circumstances. That image was Jackie Kennedy, who was always stylish and graceful, even in the face of danger and loss. The problem was, Jackie was in mourning, not dressing for a custody hearing in which she would be attacked from every quarter. Of course I could have made worse choices, but not by much. My outfit said all the wrong things: I pay too much attention to what I wear, and perhaps too much attention to myself. And it sent all the wrong messages to the judge. In any case, he clearly disliked me from the minute we made eye contact. He looked me up and down, arched his eyebrows, and turned his mouth down just a touch—all to express disapproval—and then looked away.

Remarkably, I had been saved from making an even bigger mistake! My original choice was a one-piece off-white dress with a tight waist and belt. Had I worn that dress to court, it would have been like turning up in church wearing a black micro-miniskirt and spiked heels. Somehow, grace had saved me at the last minute when the dress was shrunk and ruined beyond repair by my local dry cleaners. I was frantic when I saw the ruined outfit. Why me? Why this dress? When I got to court, I realized that the white dress would have been even worse than the one I eventually wore. I had been spared, but not by much. My choices were still wrong—they just weren't as bad as they might have been. Still, I was out of bounds enough to turn the judge against me immediately.

The actual hearing took place in a conference room that the judge used as a small courtroom for these kinds of proceedings. My attorney and I sat on one side of a long oak table. My former husband and his attorney sat on the other side. The guardian ad litem sat to my left at one end of the table. The judge, a man of about sixty, sat at the other end, behind an elaborate elevated desk or bench, much like the one ordinarily seen in court. He looked down on us like an old and worldly eagle, his eye as sharp as his talons. A court reporter, who sat just to the left of the judge's bench, took down every word said during the proceedings. Just behind my former husband and his attorney was a bank of windows that looked out on a row of office buildings directly opposite the courthouse. I felt small and exposed in that room. My husband's attorney glared at me from across the table. I looked away and then at the judge. I realized again that there would be no sanctuary from him, either.

After the preliminary announcements that stated who was appearing before the court, the judge announced forthrightly that we could "end this right now." He looked down at me and said,

"A year with you and a year with him." He meant that custody of our children would be divided so that they alternately lived a year with my former husband and a year with me.

My attorney looked at me with expectation, as if to elicit my answer.

"No, your honor," I said.

"Okay," he said, taking a deep breath. "Let's begin, then."

With that, the court procedure began.

At first the lawyers went over the details of the suit with the judge. Each side outlined its respective demands. Once the picture was made complete, the inquisition into my eating disorder—and all that my former husband and his lawyer tried to make of it— began. Not surprisingly, my former husband's very aggressive lawyer attempted to prove to the judge that my eating disorder was actually a symptom of a much deeper psychological imbalance, an imbalance that made me unfit to raise our children. He dismissed the fact that I had been free of all bulimic behavior for the past eight years as a mere remission. He argued that there was no cure for bulimia and that I would eventually relapse. When I did, I was a threat to my children's health, he insisted.

My lawyer countered with the psychological evaluations and testing that I had undergone, all of which demonstrated my good health. He brought in a series of character witnesses into the room who had known me for many years. They testified to my conscientiousness as a mother and my stability as a long-term friend. Finally, my medical doctor brought in laboratory reports from the previous four years as evidence of my full recovery from the eating disorder. He assured the court of my good health and insisted that I had indeed overcome bulimia.

"Isn't it true that there is no cure for bulimia?" my former husband's attorney demanded.

"People do overcome the disorder," my doctor said.

"How is that possible?" the lawyer asked, his voice full of incredulity.

My doctor explained that bulimia is a behavior that serves as a substitute for the expression of emotion that has been blocked or repressed for many years. The key to treatment, he said, is to help the bulimic patient translate the underlying feelings into a healthy form of communication. Therapy, in part, is getting bulimics to convert their feelings into words. They must confront, accept, and integrate many strong and negative feelings that are often at the core of their lives, but have been held back for many years. Very often, he said, a person with bulimia encounters something in the environment that stimulates a painful memory or emotional reaction—typically referred to as a trigger situation—and immediately attempts to obliterate those feelings by binge eating. Therapy is designed to allow those feelings to exist consciously. Bulimics must learn that there's nothing wrong with their feelings. Once that recognition sets in, the recovery process has begun.

"You're saying that there is a cure?" the lawyer demanded.

"I'm saying that many people overcome this disorder," the doctor answered.

"I don't believe it," the lawyer sneered.

The room was thick with tension. "Thank you, Doctor," the judge said. With that, the physician got up from his chair and left the room.

When everyone had testified and the lawyers had finished making their cases, the judge decided to postpone any ruling on my children's fate until January, some five months away. In the meantime, he ordered that my former husband, the children, and I undergo psychological testing and court-appointed counseling, both individually and together. With that, he dismissed everyone.

I left the court shaken to my core. I was shell-shocked from the barrage of attacks upon me.

I spent much of the next five months thinking about all that had transpired in that courtroom on that fateful day in August. All that remained now was for the judge to decide on the basis of the evidence. In reflecting on that fateful day, I gradually realized just how far off the mark I had been in presenting myself to the court. Here's what you should do to avoid some of the mistakes I made that day.

• FIRST, KNOW WHO YOU ARE •

The greatest security you can achieve in life is to be comfortable—indeed, in love with—who you are. When you arrive in court, you will be nervous and very much on the spot. As I have said, you are the one on trial. Don't add to your burdens by presenting yourself as someone other than who you are. More important, do not inflate your image or your ego with your dress or your behavior. On the contrary, present yourself as a humbler version of who you truly are. Wear the clothes that most suit your personality and identity, but then understate everything.

Don't take that advice too far, however. Don't dress down and do not, under any circumstances, wear jeans and a T-shirt, even if those are the clothes you are most comfortable in. As many attorneys recommend, dress as you would if you were going to church. Make a secure but slightly humble statement with both your clothing and your manner. This has the potential to move the court slightly in your favor—and slightly can be all the difference you need.

As you choose your clothes for court, keep in mind that there is an invisible line between balance and understatement and excess and extravagance. You cross that line at your own peril. The point at which the line is crossed, a point I describe in greater detail below, is different for every woman. Only you know the kind of clothes appropriate for you and how you can tone them down just a notch or two to create an understated appearance. Be aware, however, that if you cross that line, you will be making a statement antithetical to the one that you really wish to make.

This was my first mistake. I knew better than to dress in a black designer dress that day. Unfortunately, my ego prevented me from dressing down and being humble. I couldn't bring myself to appear subservient or less than the person I wanted to be. But in holding myself above who I really was, I rejected myself, my true circumstances, and my past. The obvious disapproval of the judge and the attack by my former husband's lawyer had forced me to look at who I truly am. My ego had been deflated. I was then forced to choose between who I really am and who I was pretending to be.

Healing is embracing all of who you are. There is no healing in denial.

• YOUR IMAGE: THE GOOD MOTHER •

Once you decide how you want to feel, put a June Cleaver spin on it. As I said in Chapter 2, even though the image of the perfect mother is largely false in today's world, it is nonetheless a powerful image that judges want you to convey in order for them to feel justified in turning custodial care of your children over to you. You have to present a June Cleaver/Donna Reed image in order to assure the judge of your highly developed maternal instincts and your dedication to your children. In truth, the way you dress may mean little or nothing about your dedication to your children, especially since you can manipulate the image, but you will still have to honor that image in order to succeed. Therefore, I urge you to adopt the following attitude, dress, and behavior code when going to court.

A WOUNDED VULNERABILITY AND A BRAVE HEART

The truth is that you and your children are the victims of this process. In all probability, your husband has initiated the custody suit. He has also launched a series of attacks on you and your character. The process and these attacks have injured not only you but also your children. You carry the family's pain into the courtroom. Assume the mantle of a strong woman bravely bearing the burdens of a family. You have had to put up with a terrible inquisition by social workers, psychologists, and lawyers. You've suffered financial losses. Your children have had to see you suffer. You have had to watch and bear their suffering. Make no mistake: You are the victim of this man and the system. Don't be afraid to present yourself as such.

Let your choices of clothing and accessories and your manner all be informed by this attitude.

A SERVANT OF YOUR CHILDREN

No matter what your cooking skills, convey the image of someone who spends a lot of time in the kitchen cooking for her children. A woman who's in the kitchen a lot dresses comfortably and takes a certain utilitarian approach to her clothing and, indeed, to her entire life. Be the person who, once she is finished in the kitchen, spends the rest of the night doing homework with her children. Be matronly and utterly unselfish. That's your message. Do not dress as if you spend a lot of time grooming yourself.

At the same time, communicate submissiveness and compliance—both keys to being awarded custodial care, since the compliant one is more likely to be rewarded by the court for the reasons I have stated elsewhere. Compliance goes a long way toward winning the judge's favor.

In general, you want to look conservative, accepting, and unadorned—in short, like the traditional image of a mother. Remind people that you are a mother.

CLOTHING

Always wear a dress or a skirt of a modest length and always wear stockings. Do not choose anything that looks particularly costly or that smacks of a designer label. Avoid clothing that accents your figure. Be modest. Wear nothing that is black—the color conveys power, confidence, and sexiness. It also speaks of night life, something that you avoid, at least for the purpose of these proceedings. Don't wear white or off-white, either. White is way too strong and aggressive. It also makes you look too much like an ice cream cone—young, playful, and a little too daring.

Generally, choose pale colors, those that people have trouble remembering after you're gone.

JEWELRY

Wear only the most minimal jewelry, preferably pearls, with little pearl earrings or studs. Do not wear a watch or bracelets. Avoid dangly earrings and any piece of jewelry that glitters or calls attention to itself.

SHOES

Wear low-heeled pumps that are closed at the toe. Never choose an open-toed shoe—it's too sexy and just plain unmotherly. Of course, never wear high heels.

YOUR MANNER, VOICE, AND REFERENCES TO YOUR CHILDREN

Don't let your manner or your voice appear shrill, aggressive, or overly demanding. When you refer to your children, don't say, "My children need this," or "My children need that." Rather, say "our children." Indeed, they are both yours and your husband's children. By saying "our children," you are alerting the court that you are aware of and respect your former husband's rights and his place in his children's lives. You are saying that you will honor those rights and maintain balance with regard to your husband's place in his children's lives. You are also saying that what you are asking for from the court and your former husband is just and appropriate.

When referring to your husband, be fair and balanced. Judges react very strongly when one spouse attacks the other in court, or acts with anger or hatred.

NO SEX APPEAL

Sexiness is deadly in a court custody proceeding. Do not wear miniskirts. Avoid tight tops, pantsuits, sandals, fishnet stockings, and spandex. You want to look feminine but not sexy. Remember that your appearance suggests your morality, a major part of your life on which you will be judged.

NO POWER

The one who looks like the victim is usually the victor in these proceedings, lawyers like to say. Your look must elicit both respect for your devotion and empathy for your sacrifice. No suits, no businesslike attire. It's all right to provide for your children as a working mother, but the last thing you want to suggest to a judge is that you have a career, especially one you are devoted to. It's even worse to suggest that you are a powerful woman in the workplace. If you are naturally a powerful woman, do not flaunt it, lest it be seen as competing with the judge's authority. If anything, you want to convey the feeling that you are slightly worn out by life and need assistance from the judge. Your manner says that you have given everything to your children.

He reviewed the many points of contention. He outlined again his own decision to order psychological evaluation and testing. He described his order to give my former husband time to arrange a better living arrangement for the children. And then, without any sense of the dramatic, he announced that he was granting me custodial rights to the children. Without skipping a beat, he went on to describe broad and liberal visitation rights for my former husband. He continued to speak about the need for post-marital counseling, but I stopped listening. All I could hear was his order to keep the children with me. I was stunned. I had won.

9 FINDING THE LIGHT AT THE END OF THE TUNNEL: FORGIVENESS AND SELF-HEALING

Suddenly it's over. You feel as if you've finally washed up on shore after being shipwrecked and tossed around by a violent storm. All your reserves are gone. You're depleted physically, psychologically, financially, and spiritually. You've spent months, perhaps years, defending yourself as a woman and mother. You've weathered the attacks and effrontery of your former husband, social workers, psychologists, lawyers, and even a judge. Tens of thousands of dollars have been washed down the drain—money that you needed for a hundred different purposes, not the least of which might have been to support your children's education. Now you're broke.

When you look at your children, you see how wounded, angry, and afraid they are after all that they've been through. Your relationship with them is strained and perhaps permanently injured. You ask yourself for what? So that your former husband could wrest the children from you? So that he could be the father that he wanted to be? So that he could protect them from you, their mother? So that he could exact a small measure of revenge against you? Even when you grant him his most altruistic motivation, even if you say that his only motivation was the belief that he could raise them better than you could, you are still left with the knowledge that this long, torturous, and abusive procedure did more to hurt them than anything the two of you, as their parents, could have done. You shake your head and cry your eyes out and beat your pillow till the feathers fly around the room. You ask yourself, Why didn't sanity descend at some point during this insane process? Why couldn't we arrive at some amicable arrangement for their good, if not our own? But then you realize that sanity was never a mark of your marriage. That realization leads you to the blinding truth that the two of you consistently created chaos and conflict throughout your long relationship and that this custody procedure was almost inevitable, given who the two of you are. Ultimately, all you can feel is anger, bitterness, and an overwhelming sense of betrayal—betrayal by your former husband, by you yourself, and by the universe. The question is, Where do you go from here?

• START FROM WHERE YOU ARE •

From where I stand today, having been through the healing process and having forgiven all those who needed forgiveness—most of all myself—I can say with assurance that life is essentially a healing journey. What you have to do is allow life to do what it does naturally. You have to trust life to bring you back to wholeness, sanity, and peace.

The first step in trusting that process is this: *Do not force yourself to feel anything but what you feel right now.* Many people mistakenly believe that once the custody process is over, you must immediately forgive all those people who wounded you or made you feel less than what you truly are. Do not attempt to forgive prematurely. It's no good. It won't work. It will only repress the feelings you have right now.

What you feel now is appropriate and true. You have been wounded badly by your experience. Among the feelings you may have are anger, bitterness, sadness, and fear. You may also feel some deep heartache, some terrible pain over what was and what might have been. If you try to repress those feelings, you will only create internal conflict, which will make all your negative feelings even more intense. If you tell yourself you're not supposed to be angry or bitter or disgusted, you're going to get even angrier.

Let's address the anger first. But as we do, let's say that the anger is a metaphor for any negative or harmful feeling you may have, such as disgust, bitterness, resentment, or a desire for revenge. Allow everything that you do feel to exist as it is for a while.

In fact, you are supposed to be angry right now. You have every right to be. Things went very badly in your life. You have been through a dark and difficult period. It's natural for you to be angry. The question is: Who are you angry at? Certainly you are angry at your former husband. You may also be angry at the legal system, including the lawyers and the judge and the social service agencies, especially the social workers and psychologists. You may even be a little angry at your children for not siding with you more explicitly in the process. Finally, though it may be very difficult to admit, you are perhaps most angry at yourself. Why, you may ask, did you bring this man, your former husband, into your life in the first place? Why didn't you foresee this custody thing coming? Why didn't you find some way of avoiding it? Why did you make the mistakes you made during the process?

Whatever recriminations you may have for yourself, allow them to exist for a while so that you can understand them a little better. And instead of looking at individual criticisms, let's just look at the dynamic that may be occurring inside you. When we are angry at ourselves, we are divided against ourselves: One part of us—say, the critical part of our brain—is angry at another part of us, the part we label powerless or naive or unintelligent. The angry part of us can be labeled the critical aggressor. The naive part is the victim.

On further examination, we can say that neither part understands how to create a good and happy life. The critical part knows only how to criticize ourselves and others; the weak part only knows how to suffer. These two sides of us are locked in a self-destructive relationship that most of us suffer from today. As long as these two parts dominate our inner lives, we will live in conflict. But even worse, we will not be able to create a better life for ourselves. The reason is that both sides are turned inward: one side is too critical, the other too self-conscious, too afraid. Neither has the capacity to initiate a positive action and create a better life. Consequently, they block your life energy from flowing out into the world in a creative and self-supporting way. In other words, they prevent you from loving yourself and loving others.

Now in order to understand and escape from these two aspects of ourselves, we must first keep from labeling either of them as bad or wrong. In fact, they are both parts of us that need to be loved and integrated if we are to allow other aspects of our being—the constructive parts—to grow and develop. The other parts, which I will get to shortly, can exist only if the critic and the victim are recognized, understood, and allowed to have their say. Once these two parts know that it's okay for them to exist, other parts of us will emerge.

So let's look at the critic and the victim with love and understanding.

• THE CRITIC: ALL SHE WANTS IS FOR LIFE • TO BE PERFECT

The critic inside each of us has a very basic and simple nature: She wants us to create a life that is easy and fun, full of love, self-expression, and fulfillment. There's only one problem: Life is difficult. The truth is that life contains a great deal of suffering. Buddhism's first noble truth, that life is suffering, is a fundamental aphorism, no matter what your religious or spiritual background may be. Many people today are saying the same thing when they refer to Murphy's Law, meaning that anything that can go wrong will go wrong. Buddhism's first noble truth or Murphy's Law— whatever you want to call it—is a fundamental part of life. Every religious and spiritual tradition has had its own unique expression of this truth. Christians, especially Roman Catholics, have viewed suffering as part of the spiritual path toward Christ. Jews believe that we can grow as human beings only by confronting life head-on and by dealing with all of life's struggles and suffering honestly and directly. Life is difficult, every tradition tells us.

Yet all traditions also tell us that difficulties have meaning. They help us understand ourselves. They help us develop myriad abilities and talents. Perhaps most important of all, they help us to grow up and develop into compassionate human beings. Difficulties teach us to have compassion for ourselves and others. At some point, we realize that we are all suffering and that no one escapes pain, no matter how pretty or orderly their external lives may appear to be.

Carl Jung, the great Swiss psychologist, pointed out that no one is an artist when it comes to life. We are all making our own unique versions of disorder and mess. As much as we want to impose some external order on our affairs, we find that life is always breaking through and disrupting our plans. Someone once said that the surest way to make God laugh is to make a plan. Life is too rich and unwieldy to confine it to our simple minds and little designs.

Little wonder, therefore, that the critic inside of you is angry. It keeps wanting life to be fun and fulfilling. It wants life to fit into its own orderly schemes. That's natural. Plans and order create feelings of safety and security. We all want those feelings. Indeed, they are part of what get us through the day. We can't blame ourselves for wanting such things. The critic has only one problem: It thinks that you should be responsible for creating perfection and unbroken order in your life. The critic believes that such a thing is possible. And because it believes this, it gets angry at you when things become imperfect and disorderly. The critic becomes angry when life does what life does. That is its first mistake.

The critic's second mistake is even more problematical: The critic has no compassion. This is fundamental to its character. *There is no compassion in the critic.* Get that straight! In order to heal, however, you need compassion. In fact, compassion for yourself is essential if you are going to understand yourself and create a new life. The question is, How can you experience compassion? The answer is slightly paradoxical, but true: You must experience your anger.

• ANGER IS THE GATEWAY TO COMPASSION •

Rather than repress your anger or tell yourself that it shouldn't exist, I would like you to sit in a peaceful place in your home—a place where you will not be interrupted—and experience your anger in all its glory. Get into it! Feel the anger. Carry it in your heart. Hold it in your consciousness so that you can feel every billowing cloud and searing shaft of it. If you have to, hit a pillow or a bunch of pillows. Punch the pillows until all the anger comes to the surface. If you do this for a few minutes or longer, you will eventually start to cry. There are three reasons why you cry. First, you have encountered your sadness, which is cleansing and healing. Second, you have found the victim inside yourself. And third, you have encountered the second fundamental truth about life, which is this: Some of life can be controlled and some of it cannot.

The truth is, many of the things that happen to you, both the good and the bad, are not within your power to avoid or prevent. Many opportunities arrive out of the blue for which you can take very little credit for attracting. Many difficulties arrive on your doorstep that you have no way of knowing about in advance or preventing. That's the way life is. At the very core of life lies a paradox, which is that you can control it some of the time and yet much of life is beyond your control.

The victim inside of you knows that life is out of control. It knows very intimately this one side of the paradox. And it is sad about that fundamental truth.

• THE VICTIM: ALL SHE WANTS IS FOR LIFE • TO BE PERFECT

Like the critic, the victim in you wants life to be easy and fun, full of love, self-expression, and self-fulfillment. The victim wants life to be orderly and predictable so that it can feel safe all the time. Two aspects of the victim that are problematical for us all: First, it is the part of you that experiences its powerlessness; and second, it believes that you, as an adult human being, have no power. From this condition of powerlessness, *the victim insists that life must be easy, perfect, caring, and nurturing without your having to do anything to create these conditions.* The victim, in short, is a child searching for a mother.

The victim blames other people or situations for its problems. But secretly it blames itself, meaning you, for creating your problems. Blame always comes from the experience of powerlessness. The victim sees itself as an innocent child. The bad things that happen to this child arise from external sources. That's what makes it a victim. But if bad things arise from external sources, the victim has no responsibility in their creation. The victim is innocent *and* powerless. Therefore, it has to blame others, the causes of its problems.

Naturally the victim is full of fear. It is cowering in some recess of your consciousness and encouraging the adult you to hide as well. Like the critic, it is angry, but unlike the critic, it is afraid of its anger. The victim believes that if it shows its anger, others will rear up and attack it for displaying anger. Hence, it is afraid of its anger.

But more than anything else, the victim is sad. It believes that life is cruel and that powerful people are always hurting you. Moreover, the victim inside of you believes that you can't do anything to stop others from hurting you. The thing to do with the victim is to experience it fully.

After you have experienced your anger and have entered your sadness, allow the sadness to come billowing up into your heart. Feel it fully. Cry your eyes out. Those tears are healing tears. They arise from the confrontation with a basic truth of life: that much of life is uncontrollable and that bad things happen to us, even when we are innocent of their causes.

• SADNESS LEADS TO LIBERATION •

One of the great ironies of life is that sadness, when it is experienced purely and fully, leads to compassion—compassion for yourself, first, and then for everyone else. Sadness puts us in touch with how really difficult life is. It also makes us recognize all that we have been through, all the suffering we have had to endure, and how much we have borne through this life.

I am a single mother, one of the hardest roles to fill on this earth. All I have to do is think about all that I have to do every day and—if I am looking at my life with real compassion—I could just sit down and cry my eyes out that someone has to do all of that in order to live. Yet once I experience real compassion for myself, the burdens are lifted. I give myself time and understanding. It's all right to make mistakes, to be less than some false notion of perfection. I'm doing pretty well, I tell myself, particularly in light of all that I am bearing. I feel love for myself and appreciation for all that I am attempting to do. I marvel, in fact, that I am able to do all that I am doing. When I look at my life with compassion, I realize that my proverbial cup is more than half full.

If you look at your life with compassion, you will marvel, too. After all, you have had many difficulties to contend with in life. It's a miracle that you have come as far as you have. And when you examine your life with compassion, you will see that at every step along the way, you have been struggling to do the best you could do against mighty odds and great resistance. Congratulations, I want to tell you. You've done well with all that you've had to contend with.

Allow me to make an important distinction here between compassion and self-pity. Compassion is heartfelt and honest, but most of all it possesses love for yourself and for others. Self-pity is full of anger and a thinly disguised self-hatred. If you are feeling self-pity, know that you are still in the victim part of your consciousness and that you are still blaming yourself and others.

But if experiencing compassion means that you are no longer in the victim part of your consciousness, then where are you in your inner being? Welcome to the realm of the higher self.

• THE HIGHER SELF: THE LOVER-WARRIOR •

We have to ask ourselves a simple question when we do the exercise I have just asked you to do: What is holding the critic and the victim when we enter into these inner realms and allow them to exist? What is going into these dark corners of our minds and facing all that anger, bitterness, hostility, rage, and fear? What is willing to confront the pain, contain the anger, and soothe the fear? Whatever it is, we must say that it possesses certain unique characteristics.

First, in order for you to allow your anger to exist, in order for you to hold it in your heart and allow yourself to experience it fully, part of you must possess a tremendous love, a love so strong that it borders on the unconditional.

Second, this part of your being must have tremendous courage, especially because it is going into the realm where all your fears exist.

Third, it must have an ability to look at life without criticizing, complaining, feeling like a victim, or blaming you or anyone else for the way life is.

There are many words for such a part of you. Religions have referred to this part of you since the dawn of consciousness. But for this discussion, I will refer to it simply as your higher self, the part that knows it is still connected to God.

The higher self understands the basic truths of life. It realizes that there is suffering and great pain in life, and that much of life is utterly beyond our control. Yet it doesn't blame life; it doesn't blame itself or anyone else for the difficulties we face. The reason, very simply, is that the higher self is an adventurer and a warrior-lover at heart. It knows that life is a roller-coaster ride, that it is full of danger and unpredictability, that it cannot be controlled. The difference is that the higher self does not require perfection from itself or anyone else. It requires only experience and the opportunity to love.

The higher self, you might say, is both a warrior—it has tremendous courage—and a lover—it attempts to hold experience with compassion, understanding, and love. Unlike the critic inside you, the higher self has compassion and love in the face of suffering. Unlike the victim, it has power to make a difference. Its power is to go on loving itself and others, no matter how many difficulties you have been through.

• THERE IS NO PERFECTION TO BE FOUND HERE •

What if you did not have to measure up to some false image of perfection? What if you had the blinding realization that you have done very well with your life, particularly in the face of all the difficulties and impediments that have been in your path? Could you forgive yourself then? The truth is that only the critic inside of you believes in a perfection against which you should measure your life. And that perfection is false. When you realize that only the critic is interested in perfection, then you will know that there is no such thing as failure. There is only what you have done, which is the best you could have done.

I say all of this as prelude to encouraging you to get help. But you have to have the right mindset to approach help. I want you to have a certain perspective as you enter the healing path. If you are overcome at times by your anger and rage, remember that you are more than your anger and rage. If you are overcome with feelings of powerlessness and fear, remember that you are more than the part of you that feels powerless and afraid. If you are blaming yourself and others for all that you have been through, remember that you are more than the victim inside you that blames.

You have the critic within you. You have the victim as well. But you have the higher self, which takes a very different view of your life and of love. The challenge to all of us, I believe, is to understand that we cannot get to the higher self until we honor emotions and thoughts that we consider lower or negative— namely anger, fear, and feelings of powerlessness, just to name a few. Therapy is meant to allow those feelings to exist. Indeed, in therapy we want to experience them fully and to integrate them into a larger, loving context.

Talk to someone who can listen compassionately and verbalize for you the voice of your higher self. It doesn't matter who that person is or what his or her specialty may be. He or she could be a priest, minister, or rabbi, a psychologist or psychiatrist, or a particular type of healer. Join a support group. Among the most popular are the twelve-step programs, such as Alcoholics Anonymous or Al Anon—any group that you feel attracted to. Sometimes just being with other women who are angry or hurt or sad can help you get to those same feelings inside yourself. Also, other women who have been injured and thus are capable of understanding you can be a great source of strength, understanding, and love.

In addition to getting some kind of talking therapy, I strongly urge you to get some kind of bodywork, be it yoga, therapeutic massage, acupressure, Reiki, bioenergetics, therapeutic touch, energy work, or other activities. Someone with a healing touch can put his or her hands on you and release some of the physical tension and trauma that is still held in your muscles, organs, and other tissues. Bodywork releases us from the physical tension and the physical patterns that form the basis for so much illness. These patterns also keep us locked in certain thoughts and beliefs that hold us back. Someone with a healing touch can break up that tension and release us from the physical and psychological pain that such tension creates.

You should understand that you are very likely suffering from some kind of posttraumatic stress disorder, and that the pain that arises from this condition comes not only from your mind but also from your body. All the hurtful words that were said to you and that you said to others are held within your tissues in the form of tension. Your body, mind, and heart need healing now, and you must address all three. Your spirit, in the form of the higher self, can guide you to your answers and help you heal.

Only if you address the totality of your being—that is, your body, mind, heart, and spirit—can your healing be rapid and complete.

I believe that healing is your primary work now, especially in light of all that you have been through. As you will see, healing is the basis for establishing a new and rewarding life. It is the path to self-love, because healing is essentially an act of self-love. Once you are healthier and more alive, and you feel that you have reestablished a loving and positive connection with yourself and with life in general, then you can consider forgiving others.

• HOW FORGIVENESS HAPPENS •

I believe that only after we have established a new life that is rewarding and happy can we truly forgive. The only true way to forgive anyone, I believe, is to become happy with who you are. In a way, you have to convince the victim and the critic inside of you that you have the power to create a new and rewarding life. If you go around thinking that this terrible experience— namely the custody suit—has robbed you of the opportunity to be happy, you will never really forgive anyone, including yourself. Forgiveness is impossible because your former husband or the ju- dicial system or your own powerlessness has robbed you of your future. If you believe that you have no future and that all the goodness has been drained from your life, you will be forced to exist within the victim consciousness. That is a terrible place to be for very long.

In order to forgive, you must heal. By healing, you regain your life, your vitality, your belief in the future. You have hope again. One day you wake up and realize that you love yourself and that you are prepared to meet life with an open heart. You realize you have conquered hatred. You are whole again.

You must accomplish that first. Once you love yourself, you can forgive, because the person who wounded you did not hurt you so badly as to prevent you from achieving the thing you wanted the most: happiness with what you have become.

The greatest pain, I believe, is self-hatred. Nothing is worse than hating yourself. With self-hatred, you feel outside the bubble of love—your own love, God's love. For most of my life, I felt unworthy of true love, even from my children. As long as I felt unworthy of love, I hated myself and I hated my mother. I could not forgive her because whatever she had done to me, her actions made me a person who was unworthy of love—my own as well as anyone else's. That feeling of being unworthy of love defined my life and all of my relationships.

I realized that if I was to forgive myself, my mother, and my former husband, I had to first make myself happy. I had to take back what had been taken away from me. The only way I could think of to do that was simply to follow my own heart—to know what I wanted in any given moment and, whenever possible, to give myself what my heart desired.

Mostly my heart just wants to love—to love my children, my friends, myself. I want to feel worthy of the love people give me. It is my particular temperament to want to find some kind of spiritual peace and to feel that I am loved by the universal being we refer to as God or the Great Spirit or the Great Mother. I feel today that the Great Mother wants me to be happy, as any loving mother wants for her children. The more I feel connected to spirit in this way, the more I am able to love myself.

I must say that only after I began to conceive of a relationship with the Source of unconditional love did I start to forgive myself and feel worthy of love. For the first time in my life, I feel worthy of the good things that have come into my life. Not surprisingly, as I do this, I see more good today than I ever did before. Feeling that I am loved by the universal being has made it possible for me to feel worthy of happiness. And that happiness has made it possible for me to truly love and forgive.

• A SERENDIPITOUS CLOSURE •

And then life gave me a strange gift. I use the word *strange* because at first it didn't seem like a gift at all. Nearly two years after the custody suit concluded, I was sitting in a café in Coconut Grove, just outside of Miami, having breakfast with a friend. It was a beautiful morning. I had driven down to the area to see a few clients and to deliver my children to their father. They were spending the weekend with him. My friend and I were sitting at one of the many tables on the outdoor terrace of the restaurant. Suddenly I spotted a red Mercedes-Benz coupe pull into the parking lot of the restaurant. I recognized the car instantly. I watched the woman get out of the car, walk up to the hostess, and take a seat a few tables away from me on the terrace.

Oh my God, I said to myself, it's her. I watched her surreptitiously as she reviewed the menu, ordered her breakfast, and then gave her attention to the book that she had brought with her. I couldn't help studying her. She had on a tailored business suit. She looked so innocent, so innocuous. You would think that she couldn't hurt a mosquito. Odd as it may seem, the question that pressed itself against my consciousness and demanded an answer was simply, Is she a human being? Does she have feelings? Are there things she cares about, really cares, things she could lose her perfect image and composure over?

A friend came over to her table. They chatted about bicycling and certain bicycle routes in the area that each liked. She had been to Key Biscayne recently and had really enjoyed the bicycling there, she said.

What a revelation, I thought. This woman has friends; people like her; she has another life; she can laugh. No doubt she has a boyfriend and parents and problems all her own.

My friend was talking, but I was in another world. "I'm sorry," I said. "But something just happened. Do you remember my telling you about the social worker from the family court services who grilled me about my bulimia?"

"Yes," she said. "Whatever happened to her?"

"She's sitting at the table to my right."

Discreetly my friend peeked over her shoulder and saw the woman.

"What are you going to do?" my friend asked.

"I don't know," I said, suddenly afraid and exhilarated at the same time.

The social worker's friend left and her breakfast came. We all ate in silence, but after she finished her food, I got up from my chair and walked over to her. I greeted her by name.

"Hello," she said, smiling. She didn't have a clue who I was. I meant nothing to her. How ironic: She meant so much to me, my children, and our lives. I was just a case, one that did not endure in her memory for very long.

I told her my name. Again, the welcoming smile.

"You're a therapist, right?" she said, still smiling.

"Yes, but you don't know me in that context. You came to my house to do a custody evaluation."

Suddenly her whole countenance changed. The human face was gone, shuttered by a cold, professional exterior. Was that recognition I saw in her eye, just before her expression changed? I had wanted to make some kind of human contact with this woman, but I saw that such a thing was now impossible.

"I just want you to know how awful and dehumanizing that experience was for my entire family. And you helped to make it that way. I also wanted to tell you that in your report you expressed serious doubts that I would bring my children from Orlando to Miami so that they could see their father. I have been doing that every weekend for the past two years. I'm doing the very thing you said I wouldn't do.

"You need to keep in mind that we're people you're dealing

with," I said. "We're not just cases with information that you can use to embarrass us. We're human beings. You're a licensed therapist. You should know that."

With that, I turned around and went back to my table. I picked up the check and went to the register to pay, my friend right behind me. Once in the car, my friend patted my hand and said, "What would you have thought were the chances that she would come to the same restaurant on the same day that you would be there having breakfast?" she asked me.

I laughed nervously, grateful for the levity. "I don't know," I said. "Pretty remote."

"That was meant to be," my friend said.

"I know that."

After I said good-bye to my friend, I took a walk along the boat docks of Coconut Grove. I was shaken by my encounter with the social worker, but I was also proud of myself for having stood up to her. I was even surprised by how I had acted. I would never have done that in the past. My own shame would have prevented me from honoring myself and the legitimacy of my feelings. Wow, I said to myself. You've changed.

And then it hit me: I wasn't ashamed of myself anymore. By some miracle that had been brought about by all that I had been through, I had realized that other people—especially people in power—had no more moral authority than I did. These people that I had placed on a pedestal—the social worker, the lawyers, the judge—possessed no special ethics; they were not particularly pure or morally upright. There was nothing about them that made them more entitled to life than I was. As hard as they had tried to disqualify me as a human being, I had emerged even stronger.

Thanks in part to their gauntlet, I realized, I had taken everything that they had to give. I was still standing. Even greater was the fact that it had happened by a miracle even I had not seen,

I was no longer ashamed of who I was. I could stand in front of someone who had tried to embarrass me and demand that I be treated as a person with dignity. I didn't have to apologize for my past or for my existence, for that matter. By some kind of odd paradox that I didn't fully understand, all the humiliation and suffering I had been through had given me back my dignity. And with it came my power.

While we were married, my former husband and I used to walk along these same docks. Now, as I walked alone, I realized that I was no longer afraid of him. He had terrified me for so many years that when he sued me for custody, I was certain he would win— not because he was a better parent, but because he was somehow more powerful than I was. I no longer felt weak or timid. I was more than the victim inside of me. I had been through the worst experience of my life and I was not defeated. Something inside of me had truly been healed.

INDEX